PYRAMIDS

ROCK LAKE

D1248912

The Lost Pyramids of Rock Lake

Wisconsin's Sunken Civilization

Frank Joseph

2002
Galde Press, Inc.
Lakeville, Minnesota

SECOND EDITION
First Printing, 2002

ISBN 1–931942-01-3

Galde Press, Inc.
PO Box 460
Lakeville, Minnesota 55044

Dedication

To Victor Taylor, Rock Lake's hero and martyr

About Frank Joseph

Frank Joseph has engaged in more than one hundred scuba dives at Rock Lake since 1987. He is editor-in-chief of *Ancient American,* a popular archaeology bimonthly; a regular book reviewer for *Fate*; and a speaker at the Midwest Epigraphic Society in Columbus, Ohio.

Contents

Acknowledgments

I wish to thank my good friend Walter Krajewski, whose onsite participation, financial assistance and insightful interpretations helped solve so much of the Rock Lake enigma. Readers are indebted to Lloyd Hornbostel, inventor and tenacious researcher, whose personal quest for ancient answers contributed so mightily to our efforts. I felt especially privileged to have worked with Dr. James Scherz, leading scientific pioneer in decoding our country's prehistory. I could not have hoped for a better fellow researcher, nor more eloquent spokesman for the cause, than Wayne May, whose affirmative personality was the cohesive matrix of our endeavors. Steve Dempsey was my earliest coworker in years of travail and triumph; his hard labors and cheerful faith in our undertaking made even the worst disappointments worthwhile.

HYMN TO DIANA LIMNATIS

Your image stands out in the lake. In your left hand you hold the torch of enlightenment. Its flame flickers over the black waters like oil afire. With your right hand you clasp the bow, yet a doe seeks shelter at your side. I understand and venerate your mystery, Protectress of Animals, Mistress of the Hunt. From your fair face you gaze down compassionately into the depths. You behold all their secrets. Lady of the Night, protect our sacred lake! Bless its indwelling spirits and grant us, the living, the enlightenment of your love!

—Roman priest of Diana at Ostia
late 3rd century

Rock Lake from 3,300 feet. Its sunken delta is clearly discernible.

Photograph by Steven Dempsey

Introduction

The Enchanted Lake

The most beautiful and most profound emo-
tion we can experience is the sensation of
the mystical. It is the source of all true sci-
ence. He to whom the emotion is a stranger,
who can no longer wonder and stand rapt in
awe, is as good as dead.
—Albert Einstein

A scuba diver neared the end of his routine if pleasant excursion under an ideal Wisconsin lake. Some forty feet above him, holiday boaters pulled water skiers across its surface and kids splashed along the shore in the summer of 1967.

The diver was able to see for only about twelve feet or so in any direction. The spring-fed waters were clean, but green algae hung suspended in the depths and the declining angle of afternoon sunlight created a gloomy atmosphere. With less than ten minutes worth of air remaining in his tank, he was

*Artist's recreation illustrates John Wayne Kennedy's 1967
sighting of pyramids in the southeast quadrant of Rock Lake.*

Aerial view of the linear stone mound discovered by John Wayne Kennedy in 1967.

Photograph by Jack Latourneau. Rock Lake Research Society, as published in *Ancient American*

about to begin his ascent when an enormous black form rose up in front of him and he almost crashed headfirst into what appeared to be a solid wall.

Pausing to reorient himself, he proceeded cautiously, stretching out his right hand to touch the face of a massive, inclined structure. He could make out in the half-light that it was built entirely of black, round stones, all apparently chosen for relative size and stacked up neatly into a pyramidal form. He rose over the top, which came almost to a pointed apex, and swam carefully down the full length of the structure, counting his kicks as a rough measurement of its overall extent. He guessed it was more than a hundred feet long, perhaps twenty feet across at the base and about fifteen feet tall. Both ends terminated in a triangular configuration, and, while poor visibility did not allow him an overall view of the object, he was able to see that it was an articulated pyramid, a monument of some kind and obviously wrought by the hand of man. The diver began to grow disoriented. His mind boggled at this impossible vision resting in the silent twilight of a recreational lake.

Slowly exhaling his last breath to equalize the pressure in his lungs, he rose to the surface. "See anything interesting?" one of his fellow divers asked casually from the motor launch.

The accidental find made by Jack Kennedy, a visiting scuba instructor from Lombard, Illinois, rekindled a controversy that had begun more than

150 years before. As late as the 1840s, resident Ho Chunk ("Winnebago") Indians told European settlers in Jefferson County, Wisconsin, about "the stone tepees" in Rock Lake.

My own discovery of this enigma was no less accidental. In January 1987, while researching the legend of another, more notorious drowned civilization—Atlantis—I found an old copy of *Skin Diver* magazine that featured an article about the Rock Lake mystery.

I had read nothing of it before, and its story came as a complete surprise to me. The very concept of pyramids at the bottom of a lake only three and a half hours' drive from my home in south suburban Chicago astounded and intrigued me.

"Were such things here as we do speak about?" If so, why had I never seen a word concerning them in any of the archaeological journals I had studied over the previous seven years? Where could I find out more about this unique and dramatic discovery?

I was soon to learn that there was simply no information about the Rock Lake pyramids, save among old and often sketchy newspaper and magazine accounts. In order to learn anything substantial, I had to undertake my own investigation.

But I did not foresee the years of research that would follow. Nor did I anticipate that such a quest would grow to include fellow scuba divers from four states, the latest underwater high-tech investigative instruments and equipment, a flotilla of support vessels, spotter aircraft, national publicity and professors in archaeology and geology from three universities. More unexpected were the startling conclusions that our finds forced us to accept. What we learned in pursuit of the elusive pyramids fundamentally altered everything we had been taught about the prehistory of our country. Like all other Americans, we were told that our national past went back to the arrival of Christopher Columbus in 1492. Whatever may have happened among the various inhabitants before he arrived is still largely regarded with indif-

*Geologist Lloyd Hornbostel (left) with John
Wayne Kennedy during a 1997 dive at Rock Lake.*

ference by mainstream educators. But the clues we found in the depths of Rock
Lake revealed a pre-Columbian tale of epic proportions, a veritable saga of
civilized splendor, mass migration, cataclysm, oblivion and rediscovery.

This book is a result of five years' exploration, from the muddy floor of
Rock Lake to the Canary Islands off North Africa, from the secret oral traditions of Native Americans to the lost myths of the ancient Greeks. The
story recounted in these pages is thus radically opposed to established views
of American history, a contrary position necessitated by the weight of evidence. Even so, I did not set out to prove some pet theory about a prehistoric civilization in Wisconsin. All I sought was to find out to my own
satisfaction whether the alleged sunken pyramids were fact or fantasy. In
time, the view that gradually emerged revealed a bigger picture than I
expected, a vaster panorama of long ago events more bizarre and far-reach-

ing in their consequences than I had ever imagined. This panorama of a lost world has never been presented before, and *The Lost Pyramids of Rock Lake* represents its first full-length account.

In originally seeking leads to Atlantis, I stumbled across another sunken city, practically in my own backyard—a mini-Atlantis, as it were—that lacked none of the high historical drama of its more famous counterpart. Its story must come as a surprise to most Americans brought up to believe that the nearest ancient pyramid stands in the desert of far-off Egypt, not the waters of a Wisconsin lake. It is nonetheless true that an unknown, colorful and sophisticated people flourished in America's Midwest at a moment in time when Europeans were groping through the Dark Ages.

Long before the first nineteenth-century settlers arrived to claim the land, the secret of America's ancient civilization had gone down into the depths of Rock Lake. There it lay, secure in the dark oblivion of its colossal stone monuments, for unguessed centuries. Until now.

—FRANK JOSEPH

The Search Begins

The facts concerning Rock Lake are available. One day, somebody will put them together and the truth about its sunken pyramids will be known.

—Victor Taylor,
as remembered by Eileen Taylor

The Tesch family has resided in the Lake Mills area since the early 19th century, when Jefferson County was first occupied by European settlers, mostly German immigrants from the *Bauernstand,* or farming community. Today, through eight generations of descendants, a memory has been passed down from those early pioneer days into the present, a historical heirloom that echoes a far deeper past.

The first Tesch to arrive in what was later to become the town of Lake Mills established friendly relations with the resident Ho Chunk Indians, who shared some of their oral traditions with the amiable newcomer. Among these descriptive tales was the story of a nearby lake they called *Tyranena*. The word, which they did not understand, was told to their ancestors by "a foreign tribe" that inhabited the area a very long time ago. In this lake, they said, either perched on small islands or resting on the bottom, were the sacred "rock tepees" built and subsequently abandoned by these Ancient Ones.

And, just as the Indians described, several little islands seemed almost to float barely above the surface of a remarkably lovely body of water surrounded by forests of cedar and tamarack. On the islets were curious stone ruins, perhaps tepee-shaped. However ancient they may have seemed to Tesch, they did not last much longer. In 1837, Captain Joseph Keyes built a sawmill, then a grist mill at the lake's eastern outlet. These facilities, in addition to providing Lake Mills with its name, raised water levels dramatically, submerging the tiny islands that barely broke the surface with their strange buildings. More dams in the next few years helped raise the water even more, sinking the structures yet deeper into the lake.[1]

While the large ruin seen by scuba-diver Kennedy at the bottom of Rock Lake more than one hundred years later appears to have been submerged long before Captain Keyes installed his mills, the smaller monuments on relatively higher ground that stood above water were inadvertently drowned only in the last century, when the lake was reportedly raised by as much as twenty feet. These two different inundations may be separated, as we will see, by several thousands of years. Some observers dispute such dramatic rises in water levels, arguing that the mills and dams resulted in only a seven-foot increase, so the "rock tepees" were already drowned long before modern Europeans arrived.[2] The Indian legend itself is not clear, and descriptive records from early 19th-century Lake Mills are lacking. Were the "rock tepees" in the lake on islands exposed above water, or actually *in the lake;* i.e., beneath its surface? We cannot be sure. In either case, the Ho Chunk tradition was generally known to the first settlers, because they renamed Tyranena "Rock Lake," a reference to the "rock tepees" in or under its waters, one way or the other.

The Tesch family recollection is the earliest known allusion to the structures that would baffle and challenge future generations of local residents. But the lost pyramids were to remain well within the realm of fable for the rest of the century and might have been altogether forgotten had it not been for a leisurely Sunday afternoon duck hunt in 1900. Two Lake Mills brothers

*Rock Lake's sunken delta from the aerial perspective of 2,000 feet. The
two spots near the apex are stone mounds, according to sonar readouts.*

Photograph by Steven Dempsey

in their thirties, Claude and Lee Wilson, were paddling their small boat
across Rock Lake in pursuit of elusive fowl, when they noticed that the water
was exceptionally clear. With a hot, high-noon sun shining directly overhead into the depths, they could see straight to the bottom. Due to a prolonged drought that summer, lake levels were extraordinarily low—down
by two or three feet—and most of the algae that ordinarily obscured visibility had died off.

The young men marveled at the crystal clarity of the water and the details
they could see far below. But, as they drifted slowly toward the middle of the
lake, a far more spectacular sight hove into view. Beneath the shallow keel of
their rowboat suddenly appeared a gargantuan stone building sitting alone
on the otherwise mud bottom. It was very long, uniformly rectangular, and
its walls sloped upward and evenly toward a pointed apex. As they coasted
over the dark structure, Lee reached over the side with a five-foot-long oar,

thrust it into the water and touched the very top of the elongated pyramid with its tip. Yes, it was real, not an illusion. Forgetting their ducks, the Wilson boys rowed back to shore as quickly as they could, and news of the sunken monument spread through Lake Mills like proverbial wildfire.

A makeshift flotilla of canoes, rowboats and fishing skiffs crowded with curious townspeople followed Claude and Lee across Rock Lake to the scene of their find. Sure enough, there was a strange building resting under the surface of the glittering water.

"Look at that! How did it get there? Who could have made it? The old Indian stories were right! What's inside? Or *who?*"

Boys leapt out of the boats, and the better swimmers among them dove down to the pyramid itself. At least a few actually reached and touched its tip with their fingers. They later reported that the structure was made of round, black stones neatly stacked up in an orderly pile, with large rocks at the base leading up to smaller ones at the apex.[3]

Word of the underwater anomaly reached the editor of *The Milwaukee Herald,* who dispatched a reporter to Lake Mills. By the time he arrived more than a week after the discovery, the fortuitous drought that had made the subsurface feature visible had ended with a series of long overdue cloudbursts that utterly dispelled the lake's unusual clarity. The Wilson brothers obligingly rowed the reporter out to the same spot, but nothing could be seen through the cloudy water. Thus began the long, frustrating history of these mysterious objects, which seemed to appear briefly, then disappear for long stretches of time. The many townspeople who saw the drowned structure and their sons who swam around it had their say in the *Herald,* which nonetheless treated the story with tongue-in-cheek skepticism. It was perhaps mass hysteria brought on by the bad drought.[4] But Claude Wilson became Lake Mills' most prominent citizen, as mayor of the town, and he swore to his dying day that the underwater pyramid was no symptom of popular dementia.

For the next three decades, all knowledge of the "rock tepee" on the bottom of the lake began to recede into the mists of a dubious local legend. Only occasional sightings by resident fishermen kept the mystery barely alive throughout the 1920s and early '30s. During another rare period of clarity, an angler stared over the side of his boat into the transparent waters to behold "a stone wall" rising up from the lake bottom toward the surface. Known thereafter as "Zeke's Wall," it was not seen again for 70 years. During the interim, "Zeke's Wall" grew to become a popular local expression for something that does not exist. Not long after Zeke's dubious discovery, August Bartel, a lifelong resident, snapped his fishing lines on a peculiar conical stone figure under the south end of the lake.

"I am truly sorry I didn't mark it at the time," he said, "because I haven't been able to find it since."[5]

The regret was not all his. The dematerializing cone-shaped pyramid was to become a source of exasperation for years thereafter. Meanwhile, fishermen in Rock Lake ever so often snagged their nets or fouled their anchor lines on perpendicular fingers of stone where there should have been none.

A Depression-Era generation cynically regarded the alleged pyramid as a political ploy conjured by Mayor Wilson to generate outside interest in his economically shattered town. Among the few residents who impartially questioned the authenticity of Wilson's underwater marvel was a scholar with a profound interest in and knowledge of his state's archaeological past. Victor S. Taylor was a high school grammar teacher who wondered if the earthen ceremonial platforms of nearby Aztalan might have had any bearing on things under Rock Lake. Located just three miles due east, Aztalan was the site of a forty-five-acre walled city that flourished almost four centuries before Columbus arrived in the Americas. Parallel with Taylor's inquiry into Rock Lake was the first professional excavation of Aztalan's pyramidal temple-mounds undertaken by archaeologists from the Milwaukee Public Museum.

Taylor was the first researcher to investigate the local Indian traditions, and he personally conducted a house-to-house canvass of the Lake Mills area for anything that might shed light on the enigma. In summer 1935, he hired a trio from the University of Wisconsin's swimming team at Madison. Under Claude Wilson's direction, they dove like Polynesian sponge divers after the sunken structures and found more than they expected. Luck was with them, because another drought, although not so severe as the one in 1900, once again lowered lake levels by a foot or two and greatly improved subsurface visibility. The teenage divers had no equipment whatsoever, relying entirely upon sheer lung power to sustain their underwater exploration. But Wilson had taken them precisely over the large object, which they identified with little difficulty. It was just as he and his brother had described it at the turn of the century.

To the astonishment of the young men, they found four different monuments close by. Three of them were more like step pyramids erected in tiers, a rising series of superimposed layers, each smaller than the one upon which it rested. Squarish more than rectangular, they appeared to be twenty feet at the base and just as tall. Most remarkable of all, one of the stone structures resembled an ice-cream cone turned upside-down, perhaps ten feet across the bottom and tapering steeply to a point. This was the first underwater sighting of the conical feature that was to much later prove so elusive, yet revealing a facet of the Rock Lake mystery.

One of the divers just glimpsed a particularly baffling aspect of the lake bottom beside one of the structures. It appeared to be the perfectly round entrance to a shaft some five feet across and going down into the mud floor. Several more holes of equal diameter were found nearby. The press referred to them as "Indian shafts," but they were not seen again for the next half century.[6]

Taylor presented his findings to the Wisconsin authorities, who were mightily impressed with the detached professionalism of his investigation

and were won over by the even more impressive evidence he had accumulated. On February 13, 1936, W.P.A. executives declared Rock Lake's sunken
pyramids wholly authentic. Dr. B. W. Saunders, director of the Federal Writ-
ers' Project, arranged funding through the state's Centennial Committee for
a "deep-sea diver" to search the site in hopes of recovering inscriptions or
artifacts. The "hard-hat" exploration would be supported by Dr. Charles E.
Brown, head of the Wisconsin Historical Museum, and Professor Earnest F.
Bean, state geologist. These gentlemen represented the day's scientific establishment, so Victor Taylor's triumph had gone straight to the top. Almost
singlehandedly, the local schoolteacher had thrust the myth of the lost pyramids into public awareness and, no less importantly, won official recognition of their existence.[7]

Only two months after the W.P.A.'s pronouncement, the controversial
structures were spotted from the air for the first time. Dr. Fayette Morgan
was the town dentist, whose open cockpit biplane afforded him an unprecedented perspective of regional Wisconsin.[8] In the early afternoon of April 11,
the skies over Rock Lake were lightly overcast, a condition that sometimes
allows exceptional views deep beneath the surface. Casually circling the lucid
body of familiar water at around five hundred feet, Morgan was shocked to
see the black forms of two rectangular buildings on the bottom, near the center of the lake. He executed several passes and saw clearly their uniform dimensions and prodigious size, which he estimated at more than 100 feet each.
Landing to refuel, he dashed home for his camera, then took off at once to
capture the objects on film. By the time he returned over the lake, its sunken
monuments had vanished in late afternoon twilight. Subsequent and repeated
flights to photograph or even rediscover them from the air failed.

Morgan's sighting generated additional popular interest in the awaited
summer dive sponsored by the W.P.A. Beginning at dawn on June 25, two
divers from neighboring Janesville began setting up their clumsy para-
phernalia of weighted boots, bulging copper helmets, entangling hoses and

air pump. After receiving directions and encouragement from the venerable Claude Wilson, they set out to the area he chose for them in a small motor launch. Until after sundown, the men traded equipment back and forth, taking turns diving for the pyramids. But the very nature of "hardhat" exploration made their search impossible. Forced to walk along the mud bottom, clouds of impenetrable silt billowed up with every heavy footstep, totally obscuring visibility.

The divers improvised a technique to counter the adverse effects of their ponderous passage by taking only a few steps at a time, pausing to let the disturbed mud and silt settle back down to the bottom, then proceeding for another few paces. Progress was extremely limited, of course, but the men were persistent and tried their luck at two other locations where they hoped to meet with less mud. After nearly 11 hours of exertion, they returned to shore, too exhausted and discouraged to grant reporters an interview save for a few, blunt words expressing their total lack of belief in the existence of the pyramids.[9]

Their bitterness and lack of success had an adverse effect on public opinion. Some townspeople declared that they had been made victims of a hoax and subsequently rendered a laughingstock throughout Wisconsin. State funds had been misused to go looking for Zeke's Wall.

So strong was the general negative reaction to the failed attempt of the Janesville divers that establishment professionals, initially so keen on the credibility of the structures, rapidly distanced themselves from the controversy without comment, abandoning Victor Taylor to bear the brunt of an aroused public outcry. But the lone schoolteacher was unmoved by the sudden change in the general attitude. He continued to claim that the sunken pyramids not only existed, but represented a lost key to understanding what happened in Wisconsin, perhaps in all North America, before the arrival of modern Europeans. Further research, he insisted, should not be scuttled because of a single, unproductive operation.

His undeterred stance generated scorn, then real hostility and persecution. He was eventually dismissed from his teaching post and virtually run out of town. He returned some years later, however, when, after suffering a fatal heart attack, his body was buried at Rock Lake Cemetery, overlooking the controversial enigma he had personally lifted into folk consciousness. Lake Mills' martyr to history was just forty-five years old. His sunken pyramid issue had entered the dangerous realm of popular feeling and become part of the desperate emotionalism found elsewhere in Depression-Era America.

The hubbub at Rock Lake echoed to Milwaukee, where it attracted the attention of a pioneer in deep-sea research. Max Gene Nohl was an engineer at the Massachusetts Institute of Technology. There he invented the first self-contained underwater breathing apparatus, better known today as the scuba, more than ten years before Jacques Cousteau made an international name for himself with the same, independently invented device.

In December 1936, Nohl had broken the fifty-fathom (more than three-hundred-foot) world diving record set more than twenty years earlier, when he dove 420 feet into Lake Michigan, piloting a special chamber he co-designed. For the remainder of his brief life (like Victor Taylor, Nohl died before his fiftieth birthday), his vital research made numerous scientific breakthroughs in underwater technology, particularly in the investigation of decompression sickness.

In 1939, he was chosen by the renowned Craig Organization to salvage the infamous ocean liner sunk during World War I, the *Lusitania,* but the outbreak of a new war scuttled the project. Nor was he new to American archaeology. In the same year that he broke the world's longest standing diving record, he excavated thirty-six artifacts in the vicinity of Tenochtitlan, the Aztec capital in Mexico City, "and spent quite a bit of time studying their works."[10] If anyone was qualified to distinguish between an ancient man-made structure and a natural formation, that man was Max Nohl.

A year after the unproductive dive conducted by the Janesville hard-hats, Nohl began his own quest of Rock Lake by making aerial surveys in the company of Lake Mills' flying dentist, Morgan. Repeated fly-overs in the breezy double-decker airplane revealed no trace of the pyramids, however. He was nevertheless sufficiently intrigued by the personal testimonies of old-timers who remembered seeing the submerged monument in 1900 to continue the investigation. More fascinating was the evidence assembled by the much-abused Victor Taylor, in whom the diver found a friend and fellow researcher during his last years.

Nohl began his subsurface exploration with a hydroscope, a kind of inverted periscope that allowed underwater views from the boat to which it was attached, even while underway. This method proved unsuccessful. But one day his drag line snagged a conical structure and he dove down to investigate.

"Sunday [October 10, 1937], however, I swam down in the Lung. It weighs 14 pounds, is completely self-contained, uses a helium-oxygen mixture and will permit diving to a depth of 250 feet or will sustain life in any unbreathable medium up to a pressure of 110 pounds per square inch. The Lung is designed so that a man is inert in the water—no weight or no buoyancy—and permits him to swim like a fish."

The scuba gear Nohl created was, and would still be thirty years later, the best available method for underwater research.

"In examining the pyramid, it was very convenient to swim down and around the structure in a spiral and then circle the base without actually touching the bottom and stirring up the ooze, as would have been necessary in a diving apparatus. This Lung, to our knowledge, is the only thing of its kind in the world. The pyramid rises up from a thirty-six-foot bottom to its upper base, which is seven feet from the surface, therefore being twenty-nine feet high. A deposit of ooze has collected at the base, and penetration of this with my hand revealed that the structure continued down. The pyramid is shaped in the form of a truncated cone. Approximate dimensions are as follows. Diameter, upper base: three feet. Diameter, bottom: eighteen feet. Altitude: twenty-nine feet. The construction is apparently of smooth stones set in a mortar. It is covered with a greenish, thin scum that rubs away easily and is bare in parts.

"We have been very discouraged at times—bucking the problems of drag-handling the small boats with our equipment, dirty water, difficulties in fouling drags, the icy waters on the bottom, etc., and have decided to continue the work with the deep-water diving suit. At that time, we will attempt to shoot pictures with our undersea cameras and also attempt to locate other pyramids in the lake."[11]

He did return to document the cone-shaped pyramid with his underwater camera, another Nohl invention among the first of its kind. The photograph showed an obviously man-made arrangement of closely fitted stones, "the size of teacups," but the diver had to approach his target at arm's length to even discern it in the murky depths, and the resulting picture was sadly inconclusive. So too, winter operations with the deep-water diving suit proved unproductive. But Nohl was not discouraged; he suspected that some hidden relationship between Rock Lake's pyramids and those of neighboring Aztalan might be a key to unlocking the mystery: "The pyramids in Rock Lake have had considerable more interest to me than their mere submergence, as have been the remnants of the ancient Aztalan enclosure."[12]

Nohl's underwater find was a sensation and had the effect of totally reversing public skepticism. The drowned pyramids were accepted as valid phenomena again. Now the general enthusiasm for his discovery began to transform Lake Mills itself. Owners of shops, restaurants, supply stores and all kinds of establishments began to rename their properties the "Pyramid Cafe," the "Pyramid Granary," the "Pyramid Motel," etc. There was even talk of changing "Lake Mills" to "Pyramid City." The Veterans Park was laid out in a great triangle at the center of town, and a trio of columns made up the shrine of a marble pyramid at its midpoint. The ancient spirit of the sunken monuments seemed to have risen from the depths of Rock Lake and materialized itself in the modern world.

Popular excitement over Max Nohl's personal quest was eclipsed only by the advent of the Second World War. A year before America's official entry into the conflict, another startling discovery was made in Rock Lake. In March 1940, civilian pilot Armand Vandre and his observer, Elmer Wollin, flew over Rock Lake just after the winter ice cap melted. Both felt sure water clarity would be at an optimum just then, and they were right. The fliers were additionally blessed by perfect light conditions and an absence of wind to stir and obscure the surface.

The submerged structures stood out in bold relief against the mud bottom, providing the best perspective ever seen until then. But as their single-engine airplane banked over the south end of the lake, they were awestruck by an entirely new sight. Below them, under unguessed fathoms of water, lay a titanic, perfectly centered triangle formation pointing due north. A black pair of circular (cone-shaped?) figures were side by side near its apex. Vandre and Wollin estimated the length of each of the delta's equal sides was 400 feet. It appeared to be a colossal platform shaped coincidentally, and appropriately enough, like Lake Mills' new central park.[13]

Their wonderful aerial discovery was not the only sighting of strange shapes in Rock Lake during the 1940s. Training flights of a B-17 bomber squadron that operated from its base near Madison regularly flew over Lake Mills on practice runs to Milwaukee. The crews often spotted large, dark figures in the lake and even felt compelled to photograph them through their Norton bombsights. Unfortunately, the photographs were either destroyed after the war or lost in the military bureaucracy.

Also missing from these early years of the Rock Lake story was so much as a single professionally trained archaeologist. Only Wisconsin's chief historian and state geologist were briefly associated with Victor Taylor's work, until the hostility he attracted scared them off for good. It seems strange and disappointing that the scientific community stood by without a word, as a controversy that came specifically within their expertise began to more and more engage a general public in need of definitive answers, or, at any rate, plausible theories.

As it was, through their mute, above-it-all attitude, explanations for the sunken structures fell by default to enthusiasts, amateurs or, occasionally, to professionals in distantly related fields. Not one word about the collected eyewitness accounts, stretching back to Ho Chunk oral traditions, appeared in any scientific journal. Remarkably, while the pyramid debate was nearing its prewar climax, Aztalan, only three miles away, was being thoroughly excavated for the first time by teams of university-trained archaeologists, who pretended that Rock Lake did not exist.

The trained archaeologists' refusal to condescend and confront a popular issue resulted in an atmosphere of uncertainty. At a moment when scientist and citizen should have been brought together closer than ever before by a great common quest, the gap between them widened into a gulf. The elitists returned to their private preserves of wisdom and left the common rabble to play with vulgar fantasies of sunken pyramids. For something to be authentic it had to be official.

Max Nohl had gone a long way toward establishing the authenticity of the sunken structures, and the controversy would have perhaps been officially resolved through his well-respected pioneering efforts. Tragically, he was killed with his wife in an automobile accident after the Second World War.

But the public waited in vain for a verdict from someone in scientific authority. The cause of scholarly reticence, had anyone looked closely enough, could have been found in the fact that, already by the late 1930s, talk of the Rock Lake "pyramids" represented the kiss of death for any salaried archaeologist on the payroll of a university where reputation was everything. Fear of ridicule from incredulous, competitive colleagues imposed a profound silence on establishment scientists who remembered the persecution of Victor Taylor, a mere public schoolteacher.

With the absence of any professional input, the underwater mystery was again threatened by oblivion. A post-war generation more anxious about its fate in an Atomic Age took scant notice of archaeological curiosities, and it was not until 1952 that the next subsurface expedition took place. On August 7, a high school senior from neighboring Fort Atkinson plunged into Rock Lake using a homemade diving apparatus. His equipment consisted of a common nine-inch stovepipe modified as a sort of helmet, 133 pounds of foundry lead for weights, one hundred feet of garden hose carrying air from a pair of hand-operated bicycle pumps and kerosene storage containers serving as air tanks. The stovepipe helmet was a decided improvement over its precursor, a specially fitted twenty-gallon metal garbage can. With this bizarre array, Ronald Hollaran and four friends conducted several dives, once down to forty-six feet.[14]

The search for the lost pyramids was on again! The boys' success or lack thereof was not recorded, but their innocent (and dangerous) enthusiasm demonstrated just how far the ongoing controversy had been left in the lurch by an aloof scientific community. Now academics could scoff at the very notion of any archaeological significance to Rock Lake, with high school students in cartoon-like outfits looking for sunken pyramids.

But at least one specialist felt its waters deserved serious study. Dr. Stephen de Borheghi, director of the Milwaukee Public Museum, believed that an issue which continued to arouse such passionate interest for so many years merited professional investigation, despite his colleagues' lack of support. Beginning June 2, 1960, he organized fourteen scuba divers en masse to search the lake. They swept its depths in prearranged grid patterns over the next several weeks, finding nothing.

But Rock Lake had changed since the days of Claude Wilson, when kids could swim down on a single breath to see the pyramids and touch them.

Beginning in the 1930s, increased population around its shores resulted in run-off into the water. Spillage from newly introduced farming techniques contributed to the general flow of material, until the lake's former crystal clarity was seriously reduced. Rock Lake experienced an upsurge in algae growth, generating a green "bloom" that diminished subsurface visibility and cut down sunlight from above. As Dan Nice, a member of the Milwaukee team, reported after a long, fruitless dive, "It gets so dark when you get deep down under that you don't know which side is up. We could get very near those pyramids and not even see them."[15]

The Midwest Amphibians, as the underwater researchers called themselves, made a discovery that was to prove important thirty years later, however, when they found what they thought was an ancient riverbed toward the middle of the lake. It was, in fact, the former shoreline. Had they followed along it, they would have discovered the object of their quest.

After the otherwise failed attempts of de Borheghi and his persistent divers, the academic world felt safe enough to break its silence. In the September 1962 issue of *The Wisconsin Archaeologist*, the very idea of sunken, man-made temple-mounds was condemned, because, the argument went, Indians did not as a rule work in stone and certainly not on any large-enough scale to construct a pyramid. Moreover, mound building supposedly began only two thousand years ago, while Rock Lake was at least ten thousand years old, therefore obviating any possibility of building something on its bottom. Case closed.[16]

Thus handily dismissed, the pyramids of Rock Lake might have remained lost forever, had not a certified diving instructor from Lombard, Illinois, literally blundered into them five years later.[17] A trained botanist, Jack Kennedy made better income as a government inspector at Chicago's O'Hare International Airport. Described in a national magazine as "a cracking good scuba diver," he was a highly qualified, professional observer who could be counted upon to tell the difference between artificial and natural formations, even underwater. But Kennedy and his six diving buddies had not even heard of the controversy that lay at the bottom of Rock Lake when they were sport-diving there on July 3, 1967. The visibility at forty feet was poor, perhaps four yards in any direction, and getting worse in the declining daylight of late after-noon.

Of the seven divers who had to surface for lack of air, Kennedy con-served his supply the longest, and he eventually found himself alone near the gloomy mud floor, where he made the startling discovery described in the introduction to this book. He removed three grapefruit-sized stones from the gigantic pyramid and rose to the surface with them. But in his excitement he forgot to take regular bearings, and repeated attempts to relo-cate the structure with his fellow divers were unsuccessful. The sample stones he recovered as evidence represented some of the most provocative cor-roboration obtained from the feature up to that time, because analysis revealed that they were quartzite from a *riverbed*. Their anomalous appear-ance at the bottom of a lake and in the configuration found by Kennedy meant they had to have been transported there by someone a very long time ago.

The quartzite proof, together with Kennedy's sterling credentials as a professional observer and diver, resparked general interest in the lost pyra-mids, and a Chicago diving symposium was held on March 30 of the fol-lowing year to discuss them as legitimate phenomena. The featured guest speaker was Lon Merrick, leader of the Milwaukee Public Museum's scuba team that had conducted its own search under de Borheghi in 1960. Still stung by criticism from the *Wisconsin Archaeologist* article, he professed strong disbelief in the structures' existence. At most, some glacial debris might have been mistaken for an artificial feature. But Kennedy insisted they were man-made. He had actually seen and touched the pyramid. Like oth-ers before him, he took to the air and obtained the first color slides of the submerged objects from one thousand feet. His photographs showed a black, rectangular mass in the same area of Rock Lake where he had encountered the stone mounds.

Taking advantage of the exceptional water clarity that briefly manifests in early spring, Kennedy and Chicagoan Michael R. Kutska organized a major search with ten skilled divers of the Narcosis Knights Club. Piecing together a photographic montage from earlier aerial observations, they divided into three teams and dove only within assigned sections of the lake. Positioned along a thirty-foot line, the Knights swept out within their prearranged grid, using the nearby water tower as a bearing. Despite their disciplined exploration, they found nothing on the desert-like mud bottom. Approaching disappointment, they were hailed by a local fisherman watching them from his small boat. He was a "true believer" in the underwater pyramids, because he claimed to have snagged his anchor line on their tops often enough. He advised the divers to move their sweep about 150 yards northwest from their position. Following his suggestion, they descended almost on top of a fifteen-foot-tall stone structure clearly visible in the early afternoon light.

It was about seventy feet long and thirty feet wide, with triangular ends and perfectly straight lines at the base. Minutes later, another team found a second, similar structure, smaller and more squarish, likewise thirty-seven feet down and about eighty feet north of the first target. Breaking into the wall of the larger structure with their divers' knives, the men discovered a cache of broken clamshells and a length of splintered deer bone, black with great age but well preserved in the near-freezing water. Once again, Lake Mills appeared to deserve its old nickname, Pyramid City.

Following up on the revelations made by the Narcosis Knights, divers Cathy Kasten and Richard Bennet, president of a scuba academy in Wauwatosa, Wisconsin, found yet another previously unknown mound near the center of the lake, in 1972. Shaped like "a loaf of bread," it was an ordered pile that progressed in size from larger to smaller stones, from its base to the top, a wonderful indication of its human manufacture. Later, not far from the "bread loaf," Bennet saw six nodular stones, each one seven inches in diameter and lined up in a row on the bottom. Clearly, years of subsurface explorations had not exhausted all the enigmas in Rock Lake.

The couple's finds drew fire from Lynne Goldstein, professor of anthropology at the University of Wisconsin, Madison.

"She would rather believe a fantastic explanation for things whenever possible," Goldstein said of Cathy, her former pupil.[18] As before, official incredulity muddied the waters around Tyranena's pyramids. For more than ten years, they slumbered undisturbed, until the discovery that should have shaken the skeptics from their cynicism was made on June 9, 1983.

It was a superb example of the tremendous results that can be achieved when professional scientists, qualified divers and intelligent amateurs combine their energies. Thanks to Robert Bass, a Lake Mills resident interested in the controversy, a truly gigantic and most unusual feature was located in the western section of the lake.

Dr. Richard Boyd, a diving instructor from Madison, decided to investigate the target with his scuba club members. The structure was pointed out to them by Bass, who noticed schools of fish concentrated around an atypical elevation rising from the lake bottom. The structure turned out to be as large as a two-story building, some two hundred feet long. Its irregular though beautifully contoured shape and prodigious dimensions amazed its discoverers. They were still more surprised to observe that its southern flank was formed into a uniform pyramid configuration. Dr. James Scherz, professor of civil engineering and environmental studies at the University of Wisconsin in Madison, measured the enormous object and determined that its orientation was only a few degrees from true north. Its human design and manufacture were beyond question.

Another spectacular find was made when Boyd himself retrieved the first ancient artifact from Rock Lake. Near the base of the huge structure, he noticed what appeared to be a long, straight stick projecting about six

*Professor James Scherz points toward a new sonar contact for
Archie Eschborn, president of the Rock Lake Research Society.*

inches from the muck. He pulled it out to reveal a twenty-eight-inch-long
arrow of tamarack, wood still in abundance throughout the Lake Mills area.
The man-made character of what became known as *Bass Rock Bar Number One* had been confirmed. And what made Boyd's find even more
provocative was the arrow's apparent un-Indian identity. Native American
arrows were little more than darts, because the bows used to launch them
were small for easy transport and rapid deployment. Hence their string-
pull was only twenty or thirty pounds, completely inadequate to propel the
tamarack arrow effectively. The bow it fitted was much larger and more
powerful than anything known to have been developed by the Plains Indians. Examiners determined it was used for hunting as a "fish arrow," judging from its size as compared with today's specialized hunting shafts.[19]

With such intriguing evidence accumulated by so many highly com-
petent investigators, the majority of trained archaeologists and geologists
should have at least given the matter some thought. Instead, they clung to
their rationalizations of glacial drift to dismiss any notions of artificial structures under the lake—selecting facts which suited their theory, disdaining
those that did not. And so, through the 1980s, the lost pyramids of Rock
Lake were as controversial as they had been when Lee Wilson poked at the
top of one with an oar in 1900.

The eastern flank of the Limnatis stone mound in the northwest quadrant of Rock Lake. Poor underwater clarity (perhaps twelve feet) conspires with the structure's great length (one hundred feet) to frustrate most efforts at photographing the sunken monument.

·2·

Exploration and Discovery

A ruin—yet, what a ruin! From its mass, walls, half-cities, have been reared.

—Lord Byron

Throughout the 1980s, Dr. James Scherz conducted innovative and valuable research at Rock Lake, surveying Bass Rock Bar and determining its possible orientation to the positions of certain stars in the night sky. But its unusual configuration failed to convince everyone that it was indeed a man-made structure, despite its pyramidal southern terminus and Dr. Boyd's discovery at its base of an arrow. Dr. Scherz also applied his surveying expertise to neighboring Aztalan, sure that it was linked somehow to Rock Lake. He was intrigued by a recent find at the top of an Aztalan temple-mound, a deep hole dug unguessed centuries ago at its precise center by the mysterious builders of the earthen pyramid.

Soil sample tests revealed that the hole had been used to fit a tall, wooden pole, not as a support column for a roof, but for something far more significant. Dr. Scherz conjectured that it may have served as an alignment marker oriented to some celestial event. Across the Crawfish River from Aztalan, he noticed that the most prominent feature on the eastern horizon was Christmas Hill, and his transits showed that the temple-mound appeared to form an alignment with its crest to mark the winter solstice. Putting his calculations to the test, he stood with his surveying instruments atop the earthwork and zeroed in on the predawn hours of December 21. As morning arose on the first day of winter, the sun appeared over the summit of Christmas Hill in perfect orientation with the exact center of the Aztalan pyramid. The tall post it anciently featured had been part of a calendrical device to determine winter solstice for the original inhabitants of Wisconsin, and Dr. Scherz proved that they were far more sophisticated than the dull primitives characterized by earlier investigators.

Following his discovery, the larger Aztalan temple-mound has been generally referred to as the Pyramid of the Sun. The smaller structure immediately north was consequently called the Pyramid of Venus, north being associated with the morning star at other mound sites throughout the Mississippian Culture.

Oblivious to the splendid finds Dr. Scherz and his colleagues were making at Rock Lake and Aztalan, I was investigating legendary Atlantis, the lost city described by the classical Greek philosopher Plato twenty-three centuries ago.

In 1987, while reading an anthology of archaeological anomalies as part of my research, I came across an old *Skin Diver* magazine article which described the Rock Lake pyramids.[1] I was totally unfamiliar with their story, which seemed particularly fortuitous, in view of my quest for antediluvian civilizations. While the article was certainly fascinating, it was not entirely convincing either. Ancient stone pyramids at the bottom of a small Wisconsin lake? I was inclined to disbelief. Probably, people were mistaking natural formations for remnants of a prehistoric culture. It had happened before.

*If one of Rock Lake's smaller stone structure's appeared on
land, it would closely resemble southern Illinois' Lewis Mound.*

Northern Ireland's Giant's Causeway, an unusual basaltic feature resembling
a paved highway leading from the shore into the sea, was generally believed
to have been man-made as recently as the early nineteenth century.

Unable to locate any other literature about the Rock Lake question, I
thought it could be decisively answered from aerial observation. I knew
nothing of the fly-overs that had been taking place since 1936, nor indeed
of any investigations before Kennedy's discovery mentioned in *Skin Diver*
magazine. A photographer friend, Steve Dempsey, who free-lanced for the
Chicago Sun-Times, joined me for our first airborne reconnaissance in early
March. Unknown to us at the time, water clarity was at its optimum, a lucid-
ity created by the freshly melted ice and resulting in a "window of oppor-
tunity" that only opened twice a year in early spring and late fall, lasting no
more than two or three weeks. We rented a single-engine Cessna out of the
neighboring Watertown Airport and circled Rock Lake at five hundred feet.

We saw some dark shapes beneath the waveless surface, but they were too amorphous for identification of any kind. There appeared to be nothing unusual under the crystal clear waters, and my doubts about Kennedy's report seemed justified.

Our investigation might have ended at that point, and we would have forgotten about Wisconsin's sunken pyramids, had I not instructed our pilot to make a final pass at 1,200 feet before returning to Watertown. Banking around the southern portion of the lake, expecting nothing, we looked down into the blue-green waters and were thunderstruck by the vision of an enormous triangle pointing due north. It was a perfectly straight figure, its three equal sides each about three hundred feet long, or so they seemed. Near the apex were two black, round figures. Those uncertain, dark shapes seen from the lower altitude might have been mistaken for glacial remnants, but this was no natural formation! Even our pilot was astounded.

The great triangle we were so very fortunate to see was, of course, the same figure first spotted from the air in 1940 by Lake Mills residents Elmer Wollin and Armand Vandre, whose discovery was all but forgotten by the time we made our first fly-over. Even before our airplane touched down at Watertown, we were excitedly planning our first dive-expedition in Tyranena. In one stroke, the submerged triangle had transformed our disbelief into conviction that, incredible as it seemed, a colossal man-made structure did indeed lie at the bottom of Rock Lake.

For the next three months, we planned a somewhat complex but thorough operation intended to document the subsurface objects beyond question. In early June, I was joined by a fellow diver on board a small pleasure boat cruising the south end of the lake. Sure of our coming success, we were in radio contact with Steve who was spotting for us from another rented Cessna more than a thousand feet overhead. Visibility from his vantage point was greatly diminished from our earlier observation, but he could at least make out part of the apex of the sunken triangle and the twin black

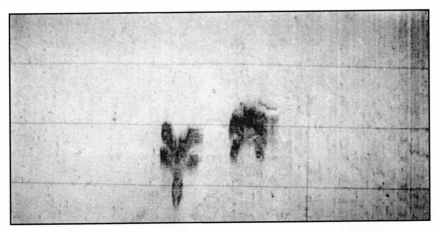

Digital images of two effigy mounds discovered by sonar in the northeast quadrant of Rock Lake. The targets are stone structures standing out on the mud bottom, but hidden from underwater photography by thick layers of silt. They represent a classic "turtle" effigy (left) found at several prehistoric sites in Wisconsin (including Aztalan, across the east bank of the Crawfish River), and a headless man. Aztalan featured the grave of a tall man ceremoniously interred minus his head.

circular objects. He guided us to a point directly over them, and we dove at once to investigate. Only fifteen feet below the surface, the supposed "pyramids" turned out to be weed beds. Perhaps they concealed something more significant, so we pushed our way into the thickly grown tendrils, which snaked around our regulators and legs. We were unable to proceed further and, disappointed, returned to the boat. Steve radioed in new targets, which he saw clearly but we could not find. Until early evening, we scoured the south end for some telltale sign of the great triangle seen so clearly from the air. What we saw of the bottom was only a vast wasteland of mud uninhabited by fish or marked by a single stone.

On reflection, we regretted not having investigated the pair of weed beds more aggressively. It seemed unusual for them to be growing in such tightly packed profusion, one set directly across from the other, unless they were attached to some feature. We had spiraled out our underwater search from the weed patches, but found no other living thing. They undoubtedly were, nonetheless, the same dark circles near the apex of the triangle that we had observed from the air. The triangle itself, we concluded, was simply too gigantic to be seen close up under the water, much like the ancient effigy mounds from Wisconsin to Chile, animal and geometric designs that may only be recognized for what they are from the air. Moreover, we concluded that the great triangle was not made of stone. Instead, it appeared to be an earthen or clay mound, perhaps a raised platform similar to those in neighboring Aztalan, and therefore all the harder to discern in the restricted visibility and lighting conditions underwater.

The following week, we returned to search for the weed beds but could not relocate them in the thickening algae bloom. For the rest of the summer and into fall, we used a hand-held fish-finder, a rather crude sonar device, which provided some notion of what lay beneath the surface. The read-outs indicated several substantial features suggesting hard, perpendicular structures. Sometimes they even resembled steeply sloped pyramids, but all our dives to investigate them came up empty-handed. What were we doing wrong? Why could we not find the targets identified by the sonar? Was it providing false readings? Were we misinterpreting the images? Unknown to us then and for several years thereafter, our simple little instrument was in fact showing us precisely what lay hidden in Rock Lake. Its sonar signal bounced off structures concealed under as much as or more than ten feet of silt and mud. The signal was unable to penetrate mud, but silt did not deflect it. When divers went down to check out its readings, they mistook the top of the silt layer, which covered the stone objects, for the mud bottom. Both appear indistinguishable at depth. It took us four years to realize our mistake, as we blindly passed over numerous potential discoveries concealed beneath the silt and mud.

Our haphazard methods were not without some success, however. Near the close of a typically unproductive day, Steve and I were drifting in our rented outboard motorboat, somewhat discouraged, wondering where to

*Divers Greg Scheel and Frank Joseph signal their readiness
to dive in search of Tyranena's drowned stone pyramids.*

search next, when the sonar alarm, which warns of a hard object just beneath
the keel, went off unexpectedly. It had never sounded before, and it star-
tled us out of our doldrums. With late afternoon sunlight slanting obliquely
into the depths and less than fifteen minutes of air left in my tank, I plunged
over the side.

The visibility was not bad, surprisingly, about fifteen feet, although subsurface conditions were darkening rapidly, painting black shadows down
below. But, almost immediately, I could discern a large, dark, perfectly round
circle. As I descended on it from above, I could see that it was actually a very
tall heap of stones piled up to resemble an inverted ice-cream cone. It appeared
to be at least six or seven feet tall, perhaps four feet across near the base, which
was lost in shadow, and comprised an organized multitude of uniformly
round stones, all black. The steeply sided structure seemed held together without mortar, and it stood absolutely alone on the lake floor.

I swam down closer and stretched out my hand to touch the stones at its apparently pointy top, but I suddenly became very frightened. I felt like I was trespassing. Until that moment, I was never afraid underwater, anywhere. I had dived with barracuda off the coast of Yucatan, at the base of an active volcano in the Atlantic Ocean and into hazardous quarries at night, never with anxiety. Yet here, in this ideally safe little Wisconsin lake, where the only real threats to life and limb came from speeding boaters, I experienced the onset of terror. Previous dives there had been entirely pleasurable. But at first sight of what was surely one of the lost pyramids, I felt afraid.

Henceforward, as much as I enjoyed diving in Rock Lake, I always experienced a tingle of uneasiness bordering on dread. Over the years to come, I was told by other divers, even long-time Lake Mills residents, that their lovely body of water generated feelings they described as "eerie," "creepy" or "as though one were being watched by somebody or something."

I surfaced, as much to regain my courage as to tell Steve to mark our position. I forced myself to dive once more and caught another, less-clear view of the stone mound in the swiftly deteriorating light. On my emergency air, I returned to our boat. Subsequent dives for the remainder of 1987 failed to relocate the cone-shaped target. Since they were first observed by the Wilson brothers in 1900, the structures were notorious for briefly revealing themselves to one or two chance discoverers, then disappearing whenever anyone else was excitedly called in to see them. Investigators now believe the mysterious vanishing act is partially caused by light currents in the lake which cover and uncover the structures with the silt layer hanging suspended at depth in a sustained matrix. Contributing to their fleeting appearances are sudden temperature inversions that affect the density of the algae bloom, together with the sun playing light tricks under the surface with passing clouds. The pyramids can literally materialize and then disappear before a diver's eyes when all these factors are at work. By the same token, the structures are only clearly visible when the various conditions happen to function together in harmony, a rare occurrence in any case.

The change in seasons did not deter our research. Steve, who was also a skilled woodworker, designed and built a large, inverted periscope for peering beneath the ice cover in winter. Early in February 1988, we returned to Rock Lake when conditions were genuinely Arctic. We had to fortify ourselves no less thoroughly against the –5°F winds than if we had been attempting to hike to the North Pole. Setting up our equipment over a suspected structure, we sawed and drilled with great difficulty a hole large enough to insert Steve's invention through the eighteen-inch thick ice cap. Next, in a twelve-foot circle we drilled eight additional holes in which we floated automobile headlamps connected to a central battery.

We knew the snow-covered ice cap would shut out most sunlight into what we presumed would be crystal clear waters. We turned on the lights pointing downward into the lake, peered through the hydroscope and beheld—nothing. Visibility was worse than ever. Some unknown debris, neither run-off nor algae, totally obscured Rock Lake. I sank a drinking glass into the water, which froze over literally before our eyes, and tried to determine the nature of the retrieved material.

We were amazed to see that millions—more likely, billions—of writhing microorganisms, some white with flexing tails, others red and shaped like figure eights, were thronging beneath the ice cap and spoiling our ability to see. We never imagined anything could survive, let alone dwell, in the lake under such frozen conditions. At twilight, the ring of headlamps lit the underside of the ice in an eerie display, but our hydroscope attempt had failed utterly.

In spring, Steve began compiling an aerial map from photographs he had taken during all our flights over Tyranena, although we could never determine which shapes were the structures seen from the air. Even so, we used his map-montage to create a grid system of the whole lake. Starting in March, when the "window" of optimum visibility opened, though water temperatures were 50°F or less, we dove it square by square through spring and summer, into fall and early winter, finding nothing, but narrowing down our possibilities and avoiding repetition in areas already covered.

Despite our lack of success in discovering any pyramids, our persistence paid off with a great find: physical proof that there were indeed stone structures on the bottom. In a southeast quadrant, a third of a mile from shore, my diving partner and I descended to a hill about fourteen feet below the surface. Visibility, for Rock Lake, was exceptionally good at more than twelve feet. The hill was topped with a rough pile of stones, all of similar size—a sight surprising in itself, because that area of the lake is a mud desert. More remarkable, the stones formed a distinct circle, and I wondered if we were looking at a collapsed conical pyramid. There were no rocks outside the circle, and its position atop the hill made my speculation all the more feasible.

We began examining individual stones. They appeared quite ordinary, although curiously spherical and almost all of a similar size. Around the perimeter, however, we found several atypical, brick-like specimens, and I plucked the most squarish example from the mud. It was very uniform on all sides but one, which was strangely inclined. A smaller stone nearby resembled a Paleolithic tool. I shrugged my shoulders in uncertainty, and we ascended to the surface with our samples.

I delivered them to Dr. Robert Salzer at the Department of Anthropology, Beloit College, expecting little significance. His analysis of the suspected "tool" revealed nothing certain beyond its "place in the local glacial till." However, examination of the brick-like example proved spectacular. In a letter of February 9, 1989, Dr. Salzer wrote, "The other, larger rock tested positive to the HCl (a ten-percent solution of dilute hydrochloric acid), although the reaction was slow and weak, but I believe it is a dolomite (a relative of limestone) and such rocks are part of the local bedrock. Further, it is my judgement that this rock has been trimmed by flaking along several adjacent edges and that this trimming was done by humans. It is not possible to tell just when the flaking was done."

We had found the first material evidence for the lost pyramids of Rock Lake. Reinforcing the stone's identification was the slant of one side. I remembered that there were similar bricks around the edge of the site we visited. In their presumed original positions arranged in a circle, additional stones placed on top of them in the angle of the inclined side would have stacked up to form a cone-shaped figure. There was no way to date the brick-like object, but its discovery far out into the lake as part of a circle of similarly shaped stones reasonably identified it as belonging to a conical pyramid of the kind described by Max Nohl, fifty-two years before.

I presented our find to the Ancient Earthworks Society at a meeting held in the conference hall of Lake Mills Fargo Library, and Steve showed the members his slide photographs of the lake's Great Triangle taken from our Cessna fly-over. Henceforward, we no longer felt alone in our quest, as other curious men and women joined the renewed search for Rock Lake's lost pyramids. Among these valuable personal contacts was Lloyd Hornbostel, a Lake Mills resident, civil engineer and inventor of the Third Lung, a device that greatly extends underwater time to divers by allowing them to breathe through a forty-foot-long hose attached to a combustion engine air pump floating on the surface. Lloyd's invention would become a useful tool in our expeditions beneath the surface, but his own participation proved even more valuable.

Another helpful find was Mary Wilson, the town historian. She organized meetings for us, helped us raise financial support for our equipment and generously shared with us her abundant files about Rock Lake. Eileen Taylor, wife of Victor Taylor's cousin, was our living link to that heroic researcher of the 1930s, and her assistance made us feel we were part of an ongoing quest spanning the twentieth century. Another Lake Mills resident, Wayne May, became the driving force and articulate spokesman of our cause through his talks before the Rotary Club and liaison with press and television representatives. And, of course, we were privileged to share our efforts with the renowned and pioneering Dr. James Scherz. Eventually, David Hatcher Childress, then President of the World Explorers Club headquartered in Stelle, Illinois, teamed up for an underwater investigation.

In the summer of 1988, we were joined by my former instructor, Doug Gossage, a master diver, who taught classes at a school he owned in Lansing, Illinois, "Goose's Scuba." One of the finest professional divers anywhere, he explored Rock Lake in a tight grid pattern through the southeast portion, where the brick had been found among the probable ruins of a collapsed conical pyramid. He pulled an extra pair of air tanks across the surface on a rubber floatation device, thereby doubling his bottom-time. Halfway through his penultimate tank and having seen nothing of interest after nearly a two-hour search, Doug glided to a rise or gentle ridge about twenty feet below the surface, where the visibility improved to almost twenty feet. Sitting atop the rise, very near the edge, was a large stone building resembling a gigantic tent terminating in a triangular configuration. The opposite end was less well preserved and presented a caved-in appearance. The top of the structure ran the full length in a straight apex of stones. Surprisingly, several sections of the inclining walls were bonded together by a chalky, cement-like or plaster adhesive, all gummy and viscid.

Doug executed two circumnavigations of the pyramid, counting his kicks each time to be sure of its forty-foot length and twelve-foot width. Then he fastened a yellow marker buoy to the top of the edifice. Years of underwater exploration and wreck dives around the world convinced him that the structure was no natural formation, despite its impossible location alone under some eighteen feet of water. We were without a boat for Doug's dive, which he made from shore, so he had to swim all the way back with his exciting news. Due to the urgency of the situation, with late afternoon daylight diminishing rapidly, we requisitioned the motorboat of a sympathetic lakeside

*Doug Gossage, master diver, leader of
the underwater expeditions at Rock Lake.*

resident and raced out to the new site with our underwater cameras, but we could not find the yellow buoy. Noticing our bewilderment as we circled the same stretch of water, a passing fisherman told us our marker had been snatched by some playful kids from a speedboat.

Mortified but determined to relocate the sunken structure, Doug plunged back into the lake, although he could only guess now where the target might be. With extra air refills and a watertight lamp, he dove until 10:00 P.M., but was unable to find again the truly lost pyramid. As so often before, it had vanished.

As I later wrote in *Fate*, "Doug has fearlessly bubbled among hammerhead sharks in the Caribbean, so the Wisconsin waters held no terror for him. His three assistants in the boat watched without a word, as he sank into the inky lake to search for the lost stone structure. Some moments after he disappeared, they could only see the single beam of his underwater light probing the black depths. Then that too was swallowed by the darkness. One of his helpers later commented, 'Something about Doug's descent was appalling. It was as though he were diving into the waters of death. We all felt frightened for him somehow.' Gossage admitted that even he felt 'queasy' during his time below Rock Lake."[2]

Before Doug's exciting if frustrating dives, our activities attracted considerable attention in the state press. In fact, we had made the old controversy so notorious that the *Daily Jefferson County Union* played an April Fool's joke on its readers. The newspaper ran a front-page photograph of gigantic pyramids rising out of Rock Lake, accompanied by a report explaining that "lower than normal precipitation" had revealed the curiously Egyptian-looking structures for the first time.

"Lake Mills Fargo Mansion owners Barry Luce and Tom Boycks said they have plans to buy up the pyramids, refurbish them and lead boat tours around them, as an attraction for their bed-and-breakfast inn."

The editor created a photomontage, pasting a picture of the Egyptian pyramids into a shot of the lake. His work was skillfully done, and more than a few people, seeing the April 1 edition, ran down to the shore of Rock Lake to see the resurfaced pyramids.[3]

Doug's encounter convinced me that we were going about our search in the wrong way, despite our apparently scientific methodology of grid patterns and aerial maps. Hit and miss procedures, however well planned out, were unable to reproduce results. We needed not only to find a target, but also to relocate it. It was not enough to discover the pyramids. They had to be positively documented and studied in order for them to be generally

Capt. Craig Scott and crew aboard the research vessel Sea Search
just before our electronic hunt for the lost pyramids of Rock Lake, 1990.

Photo: Phyllis Galde

accepted as something more than legendary. The more we learned about them, the more we felt they represented the lost key to a secret past of possibly phenomenal importance to the prehistory of America. The question of their existence was satisfactorily answered by their discovery. But the greater mysteries of their meaning, purpose, age and builders still lay in the emerald gloom of the lake bottom.

I felt sure our explorations had gone as far as they could under the circumstances of our own limitations. We needed a new direction and I wanted to learn from other researchers who had conducted similar investigations. The only parallel quest I knew of was still underway in far-off Scotland, at a place called Loch Ness.

The search for "Nessie" was fascinating, to be sure, but my mind was already sufficiently boggled by sunken pyramids in my own country without further input from a modern dinosaur. The creature in question seemed no less elusive than our own "stone tepees," and I visited the appropriately monstrous "Monster Museum" near the shores of Loch Ness itself to see the various kinds of craft and instruments used in its pursuit.

Of all the equipment on display, from midget submarines to subsurface loudspeakers that played music to attract Nessie, the most interesting device was an American instrument used with tremendous results in the loch. A side-scan sonar transmits a beam of sound through the water; when it strikes a solid object, it bounces back to a receiver that transforms the sound impulses into visual images reproduced on an unwinding roll of graph paper. I was impressed by the photographic quality of the side-scan, which located a World War II bomber on the seven-hundred-foot bottom of Loch Ness. I could easily identify its type—a British Wellington—from the read-outs, and I realized at once that this was the kind of technology we needed in Rock Lake.

Returning home, I telephoned the U.S. manufacturer, Klein Industries,[4] and a representative put me in touch with a Midwest owner-operator, Craig Scott, of Muskegon, Michigan.[5] He was intrigued by the prospect of putting his high-tech equipment at the disposal of our investigation, so we agreed on a mutually satisfactory date to launch our operation.

On the morning of June 4, 1989, a flotilla of variously powered craft embarked in a major assault on Rock Lake. Crowds of newspeople, television cameramen and local residents gathered on the north shore to watch boats laden with teams of scuba divers, underwater equipment, sonar and radio operators proceed slowly in a southeasterly direction.

All captains were in radio contact with each other and well organized by a central command boat, so we made progress in an orderly fashion. Craig Scott and his crew of technicians aboard the *Sea Search* swept the lake bottom for the first time with their Klein model 531 multi-channel recorder, and the one-hundred-kilohertz "tow-fish" played out on its one hundred meters of flexible Kevlar cable. The other boats had to be kept far enough away from his twenty-three-foot vessel, because their wakes could distort the sonar signal if they got too close.

Twenty minutes after leaving shore, Scott radioed the central command boat with news that his instruments were picking up a massive target northwest of a midpoint in the lake. Salvage work was his profession, so when he relayed his conviction that the sonar read-outs were identifying a man-made object, we could hardly wait to get into the water. My dive at that time was described in a *Fate* magazine article a few months later:[6]

"The yellow anchor line ran straight from a bright, daylit surface ten feet overhead, disappearing in an opposite direction through the murky depths far below. Following the taut nylon cord down into the green shadows, my body shuddered at thirty feet, as I crossed the thermocline—that barrier separating pleasantly warm from uncomfortably cold temperatures. Continuing a slow descent, I glanced up to see the silver trail of my air bubbles race toward the surface along a solitary sunbeam twisting through the water.

"For some moments longer I sank into the buoyant underworld, unable to perceive its bottom. But when my depth gauge read thirty-five feet, the emerald opacity parted like a filmy curtain, revealing the mud floor another twenty-five feet below. Its brown base, apparently devoid of life, stretched like a surreal desert in all directions.... Always the objects of our search—if they indeed existed—had eluded our persistent efforts to find them. But now, materializing some fifteen feet directly beneath my flippers, a colossal figure reared up out of the mud bottom and stretched across it like a paved highway. Its appearance was so unnatural and unexpectedly huge that I paused momentarily in my descent, surveying the outsized structure from my hovering vantage point.

"A gargantuan rectangle, its sides ran in straight, parallel lines, the walls sloping steeply and uniformly inward. The apex rose almost to a point, but was flattened at the very top, running the full length of the structure. On its southern end rested our anchor, and I resumed my descent, following

its line down for a closer look at the site. Its end formed a blunt triangle rising about ten feet above the silt. From our previous studies, I knew the silt
layer to be at least two feet thick. It covered the actual mud strata by another
four feet; beneath lay a clay-like, compacted mud strata resting on the rock
bottom. The actual height of the structure, then, was about eighteen feet.
Its width, judging from the angle of its sloping walls, I estimated at twenty-
five feet. Most of the structure was thus buried in mud. The narrow rectangle visible above the silt represented, therefore, only its upper third.

"I set out to determine its total length by swimming northward along its
flattened apex. As I did so, I could see that the structure was no geologic rock
heap, some haphazard remnant from the last Ice Age, but an ordered collection of round, black stones selected for size and piled up to form not so much
a true pyramid, as a kind of elongated tent-like configuration. The stones atop
the apex, however, were bigger and seemed mostly square, resembling large
cubes. One oversized cube, later referred to as the Altar Stone, was uniformly
square, suggesting human influence.

"Other strange sights came into view. There was a barbell-shaped stone
and, stretching over a long section of the western slope, were the remains of a
thick, plaster-like substance. Further along, toward the northern half of the
structure, I passed over a curious L-shaped object similar to a pelvic bone
encrusted with snails. Another fifteen feet along the apex, I saw a similarly L-
shaped object made neither of stone nor bone, but of metal, possibly copper.
I was astounded by the prodigious length of the whole structure. Having
counted my kicks, I determined that the whole site was about one hundred
feet long. Perhaps an additional twelve feet were lost to view in the mud bottom. It was here, at the extreme northern end, that I saw its triangular terminus, identical to its southern counterpart, slope steeply into the silt.

"Checking my depth gauge at sixty feet, I swam back and forth over the
structure, studying its details until my air supply began to give out. Carefully reinflating my buoyancy control jacket, I ascended slowly, pausing for

decompression at thirty feet, then rose back across the thermocline through warmer temperatures and into the sunbeams probing the water around me. Popping to the wavy surface, I tore the regulator from my mouth and yelled to my expectant comrades in the little boat bobbing nearby that we had found the lost pyramid of Rock Lake."

Our radio hookup extended to Dr. Scherz on shore. We gave him our bearings directly over the structure, he set up transits and its precise position was fixed for the first time in almost ninety years of searching. Very nearby, perhaps only fifteen feet south of the first contact, lay a similar structure in a more ruinous condition. Divers swarmed around both targets for the rest of the afternoon, although the day's earlier subsurface clarity declined steeply before 1:00 P.M., spoiling their efforts at still photography.

An example of Craig Scott's expertise in interpreting the returning signal of the torpedo-like "fish" that trailed behind his *Sea Search* containing the sonar transmitter occurred when he announced that he had located a "wall" some twenty feet down. He insisted that it was man-made, and Rock Lake veterans wondered aloud, "Could it be Zeke's Wall?"

Jason Bucholtz, the diver sent to investigate, reported back that the "wall" was indeed man-made, but by no means ancient. Unknown to us, the Department of Fisheries had earlier in the year stacked a number of cages on top of each other; they held game catch for spawning. The cages were very difficult to discern in the turbid algae bloom, and Jason got a fright when he suddenly came chin to chin with a monstrous bass. Craig was disappointed, but I felt even more confident in his understanding of the equipment, which could swiftly pinpoint a small target so insubstantial as a collection of wire-mesh cages.

The *Sea Search* moved on to sweep other areas of the lake floor for more structures. About a third of a mile off the eastern shore, the sonar registered a totally unexpected image. Twenty feet down were two effigy mounds side by side and oriented on an east-west axis, about four to six feet long and two or more feet wide. Their clear identification on the read-outs suggested they were made of stone, although earth construction was not entirely dismissed. The southern effigy was designed as a turtle; its adjacent mound portrayed a headless man. Both were among the most exciting finds ever made in Rock Lake and re-emphasized the authenticity of human handiwork lying on the bottom. Armed with batteries of still and video cameras, our photography team plunged into the depths pinpointed by the sonar. Visibility was deteriorating but still good, about fifteen feet. Even so, they could not find the effigies despite hours of determined dives in the same quadrant.

A similar frustrating incident took place near the close of the *Sea Search*'s cruise, when its side-scan clearly identified a line of five or six cone-shaped pyramidal structures standing in a curving row toward the center of the lake along what appeared to be the edge of a former shoreline. Captain Scott made several passes to verify the read-outs, which clearly showed the conical features each time. Sonic "shadows" they cast from the transmitted signal established their tall, tapering stature and solid composition, undoubtedly stone. For the rest of the afternoon, far into the evening, divers scoured the target area, again without finding a trace of the rock cones. The equipment was checked, then rechecked thoroughly. It was operating perfectly. The pyramids were still up to their old tricks, it seemed, defying modern man's latest and best efforts to find them. Actually, we were unaware of the great silt layer that blended so imperceptibly into the mud bottom and covered the pyramids and effigies, a curtain pierced by the sonar but invisible to human eyes.

Despite these disappointments, it was the greatest day we had known in Rock Lake, and the remainder of the year was spent analyzing the abundant sonar data, searching for the veiled effigies and conical pyramids and exploring the tent-like structures. I named the larger one "Limnatis," after the Roman moon-goddess, Diana, in her guise as protectress of sacred lakes, a choice more fortuitous than I realized at the time. The smaller we began to refer to as the "Kennedy," for Jack Kennedy, who had discovered it twenty-two years before.

Some two hundred feet northwest of this colossal pair, diver Bucholtz discovered a small platform-like structure. Fishing around with his hand in the mud at its base, he found a length of bone, a find that at first disappointed us because of its nonhuman identity. Later, combined with deer bones retrieved from other pyramidal structures, it would prove to be an important piece of evidence as part of a funeral feast.

There were a great many dives in search of the effigy mounds and the conical pyramids, all without success. By late June, the water clarity had declined to only arm's-length visibility, severely limiting subsurface investigations. We were determined to look through the December "window," that seasonal change when the lake "turned over" to generate improved clarity. Before Christmas, the *Sea Search* returned to Rock Lake with its sonar-torpedo, together with a new instrument, an underwater television camera towed behind the boat. But this cruise would be fraught with difficulties that tested both men and equipment.

Even before we got underway, temperatures dropped sharply beneath a leaden sky and the winds picked up, churning violent wave action. Standing on the shore, waiting for the *Sea Search* to complete her launch procedure, fellow diver Joshua May, Wayne's son, pointed out what appeared to be a lone sail at the far end of the lake. Who in their right mind would be out sailing on a day like this, unless they were loony pyramid hunters? Through our binoculars, the "sail" appeared to belong to a strange, all-white vessel running before the wind.

As it continued on its northerly heading, however, we could see that the ghost ship was actually something no less incredible—an iceberg! Snow and ice had somehow managed to accumulate to form a floating chunk of debris the size and configuration of a small sailboat. Never before had anyone seen an iceberg on Rock Lake. In any case, it was not a good omen.

The cruise began successfully enough when the side-scan sonar handily relocated the Limnatis structure, but the TV camera lowered to inspect it was unable to see much in the marginal visibility. The clarity we were hoping for had been spoiled by the increasingly violent wave action. The effigy mounds were found once more, but the signal was fragmentary because the declining temperatures were beginning to play havoc with our scanner. As before, the television camera could detect nothing. But relocating the effigies was important, because their sighting a second time confirmed that they were not just some instrument anomaly. They really existed.

Following Max Nohl's directions to his encounter with the tall, cone-shaped pyramid, we headed due south and used the railroad trestle on shore as a visual bearing. Our "fish" swept the bottom in a grid pattern as the depth increased to thirty feet. Then the read-outs began to pick up something. The paper graph rolling out from its printer had been showing nothing but the mud desert I knew only too well from dozens of dives in this same quadrant. But as we approached the position indicated by Max Nohl, a lone, perfectly circular object appeared on the read-outs. Captain Scott made another pass near the target. The sonar-torpedo shot it from an oblique angle, and the image revealed was a steeply cone-shaped figure throwing a conical "shadow" against the sound signal. We fixed its position, then explored the area, spiraling away from the target, but found no more objects of any kind—not a single stone on the mud bottom, a fact that underscores the authenticity of our lone contact.

While Max Nohl's tall, cone-shaped pyramid does indeed exist and may be relocated by side-scan sonar, it will probably never be seen again. Its position, about 450 feet from midpoint at Sandy Beach, the extreme south end of the lake, lies in a very shallow, muddy area with an average depth of twelve feet. But running parallel to the coast is a long, crescent-shaped trench at least another twelve feet deep. The Nohl structure sits at the bottom of this depression, which is really a former shoreline, so the pyramid's location on the edge of Rock Lake in prehistoric times makes sense. Unfortunately, the trench is completely filled in with silt, rendering it indistinguishable from the mud floor save by sonar, something our instruments were unable to tell us. Since Max Nohl saw the pyramid in 1937, more than half a century of run-off had spilled into the trench, utterly concealing the stone monument. The process of silting up was undoubtedly underway even in his day, as indicated by his obscured photographs of the structure we targeted by sonar.

Rough seas prevented our divers from checking out the entrenched object and the TV camera, as before, was useless in the stirred up water. The feature matched Nohl's description and location, but sonar showed it was not so large as he had reported. Only much later did we learn that our sonar signal had indeed shown us only part of the monument protruding through the silt; the rest of it, its bottom half, was covered in mud, which blocked the sonar. We nonetheless felt reasonably certain at the time that we had found the pyramid he first identified, and we named it "Max Nohl's Cone."

Another promising target appeared toward the middle of the lake, and the divers went over the side to investigate after the *Sea Search* threw out her anchor line. While the men were down, strong winds came up, lashing waves and transforming them into ice. By the time they resurfaced from their empty-handed dive, our boat was caught tight in the grip of frozen water.

Before our eyes, the entire surface of Rock Lake was rapidly freezing over. The crew labored for half an hour to free the hull with hammers and chisels as the ice cap spread across the shrinking spaces of open water. Already the southern half of the lake we had just visited was entirely covered.

At last the hull cracked and crunched free, and Captain Scott raced for the north shore. Three-foot waves tossed spray at our forward wind screen, which froze over, immobilizing the wipers. Frontal visibility was no longer possible, and then the side panels also turned translucent with ice.

Maneuvering entirely by directions shouted from his lookouts hanging off the gunwales into the freezing wet wind, Scott blindly and skillfully steered the *Sea Search* past dangerous rocks into the landing slip. By the time our vessel was hoisted back onto her trailer, Rock Lake's ice cap almost completely covered its surface.

Hoping its eighteen-inch thickness had quieted subsurface conditions sufficiently to allow for reasonable clarity, Doug Gossage returned to the lake in February 1990. He was joined by a team of hearty souls trailing an Alaskan dog sled to haul our equipment across the frozen water for an ice dive. He found the Limnatis pyramid again, while Dr. Scherz, skiing out on the ice cap, set up transits to fine-tune his calculations for the precise position and alignment of the structure, information necessary to determine its astronomical orientations, if any. But underwater visibility was worse than anticipated, and the purpose of the dive, to get first-rate still photographs of the pyramids, was not achieved. The microorganisms that prevented Steve Dempsey's hydroscope from functioning returned but stayed within ten feet of the surface. We never could quite understand why the lake was so cloudy at this time of year.

Our activities in Rock Lake over the past several months received extensive news-media attention throughout Wisconsin. Even the Associated Press carried nationwide bulletins about our side-scan sonar expeditions. The producers of a nationally syndicated television program, *Unsolved Mysteries* (NBC), contacted Wayne May. They wanted to see our operation first-hand, so they sent a film crew and a pair of directors to join the next cruise of the *Sea Search* in March. The forces we assembled were even larger than those of the 1989 flotilla, with ten vessels and twenty-two divers, in addition to the underwater camera and side-scan equipment, and supplemented by a spotter airplane filled with photographers.

We were gratified to make some new discoveries in front of the cameras of the *Unsolved Mysteries* crew: A hitherto undiscovered stone mound,

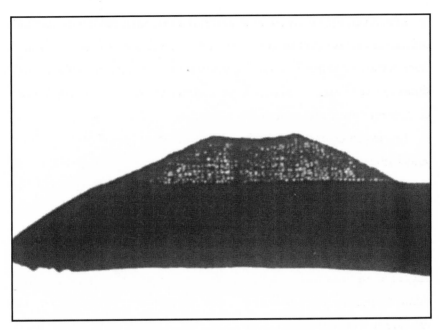

Artist's rendition of the Knob, Rock Lake's volcano-like stone family crypt.

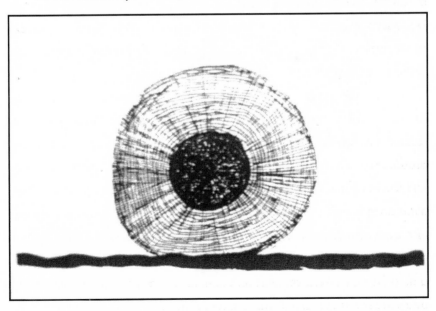

Overview of the Knob. The deceased were interred in its walls, while surviving relatives mediated on the dead surrounding them in the center depression or "vision-quest pit."

rounded with steep sides, more like a volcano without a crater than a real cone, although roughly conical. Fifteen-foot visibility allowed us to see its rise to about six yards from the bottom. No "cement" substance was found on its flanks, but the rounded uniformity of its assembled stonework assured most unbiased observers of its identity as a man-made structure.

We were further convinced when one of Doug Gossage's divers, probing blindly with his fingers into the stones, retrieved a very human-looking bone. Everyone was excited about the find, so we radioed to shore for a medical doctor and our rubber zodiac was dispatched to fetch him. When Dr. Manfred Effenhauser arrived aboard our central command boat, no one spoke a word as he scrutinized the bone. He thought it was nonhuman, but could not be sure. Later analysis at the University of Wisconsin in Madison showed that it belonged to the knuckle of a deer.

Far from disappointed, Doug returned to Rock Lake the following week with a *socouffe*—literally, an underwater vacuum cleaner, a suction device used to sift heavier objects from unwanted debris. He planned to vacuum the same pyramid in which the deer bone had been found. We thought then that the bone might have been left over from a feast of some kind, perhaps funereal, so we hoped the socouffe might recover a genuine artifact. But the long hose extending high overhead to its pump aboard our vessel could not cope with the omnipresent silt, which billowed up in impenetrable clouds of muck.

We devoted the remainder of the year to photographing the sunken structures, and in this effort we were almost totally unsuccessful, mostly because the normally poor water clarity did not allow us to get back far enough to shoot the subjects in their entirety. The same dilemma had bedeviled Max Nohl as long ago as 1937. But strides in underwater photography since then were still unable to overcome the algae bloom and super-abundant silt that obscured visibility.

November 3, Lloyd Hornbostel, who knows Rock Lake better than any-one, directed me to what he thought might be a former shoreline in the southeast end. Within a few minutes of hitting the water, I found a sharply defined drop-off and followed it until I came upon an old stream bed. Sur-prised at this new find, I swam along its ridge. A few kicks later, I saw a totally new and unusual building perched on the southern bank. Made entirely of piled, unmortared, rounded stones, all of generally the same size, was a uniformly circular figure. Its walls sloped steeply at about a fifty-degree angle.

I rose over them to the top, which culminated in a large crater deep enough to hold a man. The depression was evenly and nicely molded, lending the structure a sculpted appearance. I swam over and around the volcano-like mound several times. Its diameter was about twenty feet; its height was less than seven feet, only twelve feet beneath the water's surface. The crater seemed about five feet deep and seven feet across. I guessed that at least the bottom third was hidden under the mud. Given the slope of the figure's inclining walls, its base may have been thirty feet across. A heavy overcast resulted in unfavorable lighting conditions and none of my photographs were very con-vincing. But I felt grateful to Tyranena's guardian-spirit for allowing me this glance at one of its best kept secrets.

Remarkably, the very next day, I saw the same monument on dry land. While I was visiting with Wayne May, who had since moved to Colfax, not far from the Wisconsin-Minnesota border, he brought me to an Indian cemetery in neighboring Dunn County. The site was located on a high hill and featured dozens of mounds identical in virtually every respect to the structure I had seen twenty-four hours before at the bottom of Rock Lake. They differed only in that they were made of earth instead of stone. Similar earthworks were allegedly found in other parts of the state, but the Dunn County examples are the only known survivors. They are special graves, more like family crypts, in which relatives were interred within the circular walls. Living descendants in

*Douglas Gossage descends through the ice of Rock
Lake in a wintertime search for the sunken pyramids.*

search of a vision-quest and personal communication with the spirits of the
departed would sit and often sleep in the crater-like depression during fasts
and meditations. Around them were the remains of their loved ones, who
sometimes spoke to them through dreams. I was sure the Rock Lake look-alike
was such a specially designed sacred center and that both sites were the results
of a common culture belonging to the same people.

The question of the identity of those people was made all the more
intriguing by the resemblance of the Dunn County and Rock Lake mounds
to similar features in ancient Europe. The *abaton* was a small, round pit dug
into the ground and excavated around in the shape of an inclined donut.
Into this earthwork persons seeking spiritual revelation would meditate or
sleep, during which they hoped to receive healing visions of the Otherworld.
Abatons were used in pre-classical Greece and along the western shores of
Asia Minor throughout the Aegean Bronze Age. Some were still visited as
late as the Roman era.[7] Their similarity in both form and function to the
Dunn County and Rock Lake vision-quest mounds represents another
provocative theme linking prehistoric Wisconsin to the European world in
the centuries before the Trojan War in the second millennium B.C.

·3·

The Veil Parts

When you have eliminated the impossible, whatever remains, however improbable, must be the truth.
—*Sherlock Holmes*

Our first dives in 1991 were spent in fruitless searches for the volcano-shaped grave-mound I had found the previous November. We had failed to mark its precise location and were overconfident about our dead reckoning. But by July, we simplified and improved our procedures and quickly made one spectacular find after another. Instead of trying to coordinate fleets of surface vessels loaded with teams of scuba divers, we limited ourselves to a three-man crew. While Robert Dauffenbach, an observer for Wisconsin's Department of Natural Resources and the most skillful navigator I have ever known, manned the wheel of his pontoon boat, Lloyd Hornbostel operated the Eagle Magna sonar,[1] equipped with a superb imager that gave a detailed picture of contacts on the bottom. I was already suited up, so the moment a target came on screen, I would

49

go over the side. We thus not only saved time for extended dives, but minimized boat-drift from the object, making contact all the faster and surer.

Less than fifteen minutes out on Rock Lake using our new tactics, Lloyd was able to direct me to a structure identical to the volcano-shaped monument I had found the previous year, only about twice as large. This target was unknown to us and I was thrilled by its prodigious size and even construction. The crater-like depression could easily hold several people at a time, and I guessed the whole feature measured at least thirty feet across. It appeared to stand about thirteen feet out of the mud, although its base was lost in the concealing silt. Visibility was good, allowing me a fine view of most of the structure. How many bodies were buried in its walls, I could not guess.

Later that same day, north of the lake's midpoint, the sonar showed what looked like a wall only twelve feet below. I dove to investigate what did indeed seem like a rough stone wall inclined against the drop-off. Was it the legendary Zeke's Wall? I swam along its eastern edge, which ran in a very straight north-south line. While wondering if it was a natural formation or not, I gradually became aware of a change taking place all around me. The visibility expanded in all directions, as though the water were being purified, and I suddenly realized that I was looking at more than thirty feet of Zeke's Wall at a time. To my left, the drop-off fell abruptly down to the deepest point in Rock Lake, about ninety feet. I was amazed to see forty, sixty, maybe one hundred feet straight ahead! I paused stationary at the drop-off to assure myself that I was seeing properly. Incredibly, the lake was almost transparent and it seemed I could almost look across to the opposite shore. The sudden contrast after years of groping through arms-length visibility was shocking.

Below me, the waters turned blacker than the blackest midnight and they were extremely cold, colder than I had ever experienced them before. But I was certain then that they were responsible for the astounding clarity in this otherwise cloudy lake. When they met with the warm upper waters, a temperature inversion took place, sinking all the suspended matter. Winter had lingered longer than usual, perhaps leaving a deposit of frigid waters in a pocket at the bottom that had never warmed up. The unprecedented visibility showed me something no less valuable than a pyramid and explained why divers could not always make contact with targets picked up by sonar. For the first time, I saw the contrast between the silt layer and the mud bottom. We had never been able to tell the difference in the conditions of poor clarity that normally prevailed because mud and silt so closely resemble each other. What we mistook for the mud bottom was actually the top of the silt layer in most cases. And the structures we did find were only just protruding their uppermost portions above that layer; the bulk of their mass lay concealed in silt and mud. Sonar signals pierced the silt to produce echolocation on a standing object, but when divers were directed to the precise position of the target, they were unable to see it because the silt, which they mistook for the mud bottom, covered the contact.

Obviously, underwater conditions in Rock Lake had changed drastically since the days of Max Nohl. Decades of run-off contributed greatly to the silt and mud layers, thickening and expanding them, until they began hiding the structures. I noticed, too, the evidence of a current on the shifting silt. Nohl also mentioned this subsurface current, very rarely encountered since his reports made in the late 1930s. It plays its role in revealing and concealing again the monuments glimpsed fleetingly by divers, as the subtle current sweeps away silt from a structure and then recovers it in an ongoing movement of the shifting matrix.

Taking advantage of the miraculous clarity, I explored the bottom, finding nothing of particular interest until I heard a distinct "thud!" Dismissing it as the result of some surface activity, I heard it again, only this time it seemed to come from *beneath* me. Swimming about six feet over the floor, I looked down to see a large puff of mud erupt suddenly in a cloud accompanied by yet another thud. Moments later, a second cloud exploded with the same sound, about ten feet ahead. Were they caused by gases trapped in the silt, or the peculiar action of fresh water springs? I had never before encountered such a phenomenon in any other body of water, and thought of the swampy outgassing of bubbles associated in many cultures with dragon lairs. As so often before, I felt I was being watched, this time from the direction of the ninety-foot drop-off, still black and cold as death.

Nearing the close of my interesting dive, I swam over a very large, perfectly circular hole in the otherwise vacant mud bottom. It was some ten feet across, but I could not gauge its depth, because silt was filling it in. The hole was not far from the stone wall I had visited earlier. Others of various sizes have been reported before, always in proximity to a stone structure, even as far back as 1935, when Victor Taylor's divers sighted "Indian shafts" on the bottom. If they are the results of natural forces, no one can explain the phenomenon responsible. They reminded me of the mining pits dug straight down into the earth by the ancient copper miners of the Upper Peninsula. In view of Aztalan's important role as an outpost and clearinghouse for the pre-Columbian copper trade, it may be possible that the holes in the floor of Rock Lake were barrow pits dug to mine some material that was used in building the pyramidal structures, which seem invariably close by.

Unprecedentedly fine visibility continued through the summer, providing us with superb views of the Limnatis and other large structures on the bottom. It was precisely their great size, however, which frustrated our efforts to film them because of the distortion factor inherent in underwater photography. But before autumn, our luck improved dramatically. The Eagle Magna sonar showed some small but regular anomalies at the edge of the drop-off, near the center of the lake, so I went down to check them out. I saw what resembled a little stone chimney just protruding through the silt matrix held suspended at twenty feet down like a greenly opaque diaphragm. Lloyd followed me under and spotted what looked like stone circles in the same vicinity.

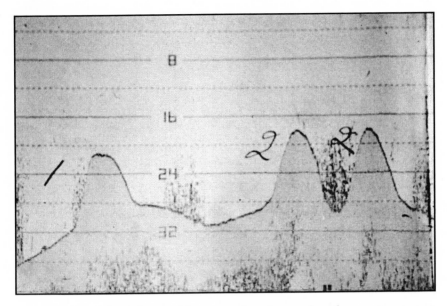

Sonar image of three cone-shaped mounds under
sixteen feet of water in the western quadrant of Rock Lake.
Image courtesy Wayne May

Over the next few days, we compared our photographs of the barely visible objects and decided to concentrate our dives in a narrow field defined by the sonar. Its signal swept the edge of the drop-off from thirteen to eighteen feet below the surface. Ten minutes into our hunt, half a dozen solid, vertical contacts resembling towers standing in a curved row marched across the screen. Our position was the same occupied by the *Sea Search* two years before, when its side-scan sonar detected a line of cone-like objects along the old shoreline. For days and weeks after that first contact, divers had combed the targeted bottom area, finding nothing. Captain Scott had checked and rechecked his instruments; they were functioning perfectly. Wondering if we were in for a rerun of 1989's frustrating mystery, we plunged through a layer of emerald-colored algae bloom hanging suspended at a depth of about eight feet that drastically cut down the subsurface sunlight. But below it, water clarity was still good, although gloomy with shadow. We split up at the eighteen-foot drop-off. I went south and almost at once came upon a semicircle of arranged stones rising just above the silt matrix, which kept me from getting very near. One inadvertent kick with a fin and rising silt would spoil the delicate visibility for the rest of the dive.

I continued south, wondering at the remarkable clarity so unusual for Rock Lake in August, or in any month for that matter. Less than twenty feet from the semicircle, I gasped into my regulator at the sudden appearance beneath me of a huge and very obviously man-made, apparently perfect circle of gray, undressed stones. It seemed to lie flat, but on closer inspection it rose less than a foot above the silt layer. Large stones ringed the perimeter as though laid out by a compass: They got smaller toward the middle, which had a center point comprising a single stone. The circle was at least seven feet in diameter. Again, I could not risk getting too close because of the ultrasensitive silt, but my hovering, overhead views of the structure were wonderful. Not so my photographs, which suffered in the inadequate light conditions. The distortion factor blotted out all contrasts in so large a subject. (Flash was useless because it only reflected back particles suspended in the water.)

Lloyd had far better luck. Traveling north along the old shoreline on his Third Lung invention, he found what appeared to be a round tower of fitted stones, some of them quite hefty, rising more than three feet out of the silt. The structure showed no evidence of "cement" or any bonding material, but looked as if the stones had been stacked up somehow and balanced to maintain the shape. It was by no means a simple rock pile, but a well-made, carefully constructed circular wall encompassing a hollow space. I reached in through the open top and felt a solid layer or floor that I guessed to be about two feet within the edifice. In the decent visibility, we could clearly see that the walls widened down from the top in a slope that continued on through the silt, where the majority of the structure was lost to view.

Lloyd Hornbostel gets a fix on our position
directly over the line of underwater stone structures.

Lloyd very slowly and carefully felt with his hand beneath the suspended silt matrix, just as Max Nohl had done fifty-four years before, blindly following the slope of the wall as it extended deeper toward the mud bottom, which he could not reach. From this investigation, however, we were able to determine the rounded cone shape of the figure and an approximation of its height, between six and seven feet. If it is standing on the old mud bottom, a total original height of twelve to fifteen feet is not unrealistic. Its stones protruding above the silt layer belong only to the uppermost section or apex.

One especially attracted our attention. It was bright red with strong hues of brilliant orange running through it, giving it a flame-like quality which was, unfortunately, almost entirely washed out in our photography. About the size and shape of a softball, the only one of its kind rests near the top of the pyramidal cone. In five consecutive summers of diving Rock Lake, I never came across anything like it before. This unique stone mystified us until a Lake Mills antiquarian and member of the Ancient Earthworks Society identified it from our photographs and description as *hixtonite,* a trace-mineral containing elements of copper responsible for its fiery glow.

Outside of occasional deposits around Lake Erie and in Minnesota, the nearest source for the mineral is Hixton, Wisconsin, about 140 airline-miles away. Hixtonite does not occur naturally in Rock Lake, so its existence there can only mean it must have been imported. Our specimen's discovery as part of the sunken structure is highly significant, because hixtonite is known to have been used by prehistoric peoples of the Mississippian culture—the so-called "Mound Builders"—as a ceremonial mineral in the manufacture of religious ornaments, sacred arrowheads and ritual drill bits. It was displayed as a decorative stone of spiritual power, regarded as holy and exported throughout the Midwest, down into the Deep South, as far as Florida and the Gulf Coast. Several Iroquois tribes and those who spoke Sioux dialects—such as the Ho Chunk, Yuchi, and Menomonie—still preserve traditions of Rock Lake with its underwater City of the Dead. Another such tribe is the Oneida, who call themselves the "People of the Stone." The title refers to their forefathers' gift of a sacred red stone, a hallowed talisman linking the Oneida to their ancient origins.

The "red stone" found in 1991 appears to have been especially imported from Hixton as an ornamental-ceremonial inclusion in the underwater monument, and may have formed a continuous ring or band mostly around the upper part. In any case, the presence of hixtonite in the stone pyramid is a valuable contribution to the establishment of its authenticity. Lloyd's find, as stirring as it was, generated new questions. What accounted for its ragged top? Had the peak been ruined in the course of time, or was the structure specially designed with an open apex? We remembered the often told tales of fishermen who snagged their nets and anchor lines on unac-

Side-scan sonar picks up five conical stone mounds in a line curving along the "Drop Off" under the western quadrant of Rock Lake. Their cone shape appears in the white sound "shadows" streaming from each target. The straight white line at the bottom represents the wake of our sonar-boat.

countable "rock piles" rising vertically from the middle of the lake. Had these chance encounters pulled off the peak of the cone-shaped pyramid?

After our first encounter with the underwater "chimneys," the same antiquarian who had identified the hixtonite told me that he already knew about the chimneys from Yuchi tribal elders, via an intermediary. He was informed that the Yuchi not only preserved old oral traditions about the sunken stone shrines, but the Indians knew that their apexes were broken off. Remarkably, he informed me of this Native American description before I could tell him that the structures we saw all appeared to have had their peaks roughly removed. He went on to say that the Yuchi believe the pyramid tops were intentionally destroyed for ritual reasons before being abandoned, to deconsecrate the sacred precinct and prevent desecration by nonbelievers. This wonderful folk memory showed that the prehistoric monuments drowned in Rock Lake were still alive in the tribal consciousness of contemporary Native Americans, who were willing to disclose at least part of what they knew about them. It also compliments the mass evacuation of Aztalan in A.D. 1320 and the suspected, artificially created flood that sank the pyramids many centuries earlier.

We were also aware of that comparable assembly of cement-cones covered with domes of earth and lining the ridge overlooking Aztalan itself. Their tops were hollow, too, while stone floors once supported tall alignment posts that marked the positions of sun, moon, stars and constellations. Was the sunken conical structure part of that astronomical complex? These questions were not answered by additional finds made through September, when Lake Mills diver Greg Scheel found another tower-like feature, although much smaller, about the size of a human head. Together with Lloyd and myself, the three of us located five or six similar monuments of various sizes and states of preservation. All were laid out in a rough line from thirteen to eighteen feet beneath the surface, precisely along the old shoreline that was above water even before Aztalan was a thriving ceremonial center. Their number, arrangement and position corresponded exactly to read-outs made by Craig Scott's side-scan instruments two years earlier. We were extremely fortunate to find them now only because of the lingering cold pocket of winter water drawing back the veil of suspended silt that normally hid the pyramids from view. And although our precise bearings would in the future enable us to return to their exact position, we would be lucky to ever actually see them again, after the silt curtain was pulled over the structures once more.

In September, Steven Hackenberger, professor of anthropology at the University of Wisconsin (Rock County), dove with us using the Third Lung to examine one of the "chimneys" first hand. The exceptional visibility with which we had been blest all summer was rapidly being overcome by spreading algae bloom, and we could see little more than six feet in any direction.

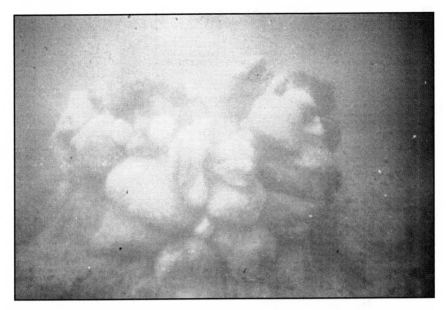

Side view of a stone structure found in the western quadrant of Rock Lake. Enigmatically known as Pokasawa pits *to the Ho Chunk Indians, they once formed a line of many hundred such monuments from the lake to Michigan's Upper Peninsula, where a few still exist. They thus connected Rock Lake with the ancient copper mining industry.*

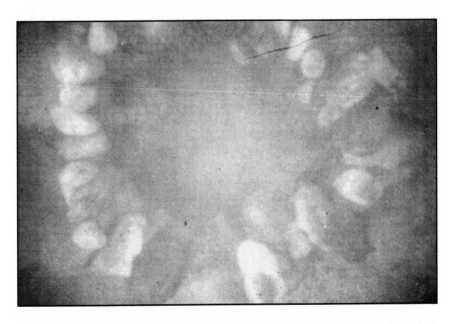

Overhead view of a stone structure found in the western quadrant of Rock Lake reveals its hollow interior.

Conditions had deteriorated so badly that we were unable to relocate any of the remarkable structures until I spotted a circular stone wall unknown to us.

Somewhat broader than the others we had seen and in a more ruinous state of preservation (one section was almost completely collapsed), it was nonetheless in sufficiently good shape for Dr. Hackenberger to observe its man-made character. It, too, rose like the top of a cone-like pyramid poking its uppermost section above the silt layer. Some of the stones were larger than any we had noticed before. Several examples might have weighed fifty pounds or more. Like the others, the apex appeared to have been ripped off and the inside was hollow.

At twenty feet below the surface, the tower-like feature was also the deepest of our related discoveries along the drop-off. The find was additionally significant in that it represented the sixth such contact made on the old shoreline and corresponded to the six solid vertical targets throwing cone-shaped sonic shadows by the side-scan sonar in 1989. It was important for Dr. Hackenberger to see for himself the man-made character of the "chimney," because we wanted to convince the State of Wisconsin authorities that Rock Lake was worth protecting as a valuable historic site.

On the afternoon we first photographed the little towers, I swam back over the largest circle that had so impressed me and noticed a gray, roughly triangular stone lying about fifteen feet from the structure. It attracted my attention because it was unlike all the other blackish, rounded rocks. Prying it out from the lake bottom, I saw nothing more unusual about the stone's otherwise ordinary appearance, save for one side that was untypically indented. Although it was an encumbrance hardly worth the effort to retrieve it, I must have brought it back up to the surface and placed it in the boat. I write "must have," because I do not remember doing so. Was I low on air without realizing my diminished tank pressure and not getting enough oxygen to my brain? Had I somehow spaced out into a trance? Maybe I was just more fatigued by the day's excite-

*Dr. Steve Hackenberger uses the Third Lung
to dive on one of Rock Lake's sunken structures.*

*The Third Lung device that participated in our
underwater search for the sunken structures of Rock Lake.*

ment and exertions than I realized. In any case, I only remember seeing the wedge-shaped stone on the bottom and picking it up. I have no recollection of carrying it or placing it on deck.

Rationalizing my fatigue, I carried the stone around in my car for part of a week, hardly giving it another thought. A few days after my dive, I set it up in bright sunlight for a photograph, as I did most of our finds, regardless of their apparent significance or lack thereof. While readying my camera, someone behind me asked, "Why is that old ship carved on the stone?" Unable to understand what he meant, I stood with him about ten feet back from the specimen. In the early afternoon light, I was astonished to make out easily the clear outline of a vessel's hull, its high stem-posts at bow and stern curved in the manner of a ship from the ancient world. There were shields, portholes, or oar holes in a line below the gunwale, and waves lapped the side boards. I could even distinguish the mast with its square sail. Even so, it was too much to believe. Our imaginations must have run away with us; that was all. But my friend did not know that the stone was from Rock Lake.

Someone else entered the room and, without prompting, identified the image: "It's an old sailing ship." Most persons who saw the stone perceived the same vessel. A single observer thought it looked more like a duck. (There's one in every crowd.) But my rational mind staggered at the possibility of a ship's representation. I could not deny, however, that the image featured many details in common with representations of Bronze Age vessels from Phoenicia, Troy, Minoan Crete and Mycenaean Greece. The stone was also unusual, certainly untypical, for the deep, crescent indentation that included the image. It had to be a simulacrum, a result of fortuitous natural forces that just happened to carve the likeness of a ship of the kind that came to this part of the world in the ancient past. On reflection, that, too, seemed unbelievable. And even if I wholeheartedly accepted such a rationalization,

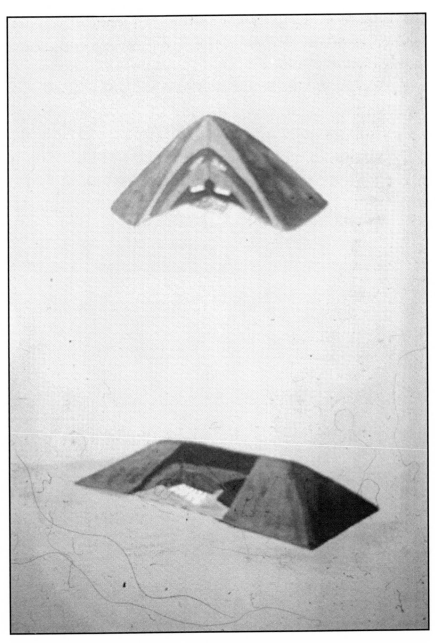

Cutaway illustration of Rock Lake structures. Top: alternating layers of gravel, clay, and river-bed stones rise in a conical configuration over the graves of ruling family members. Bottom: The Limnatis ridge-top burial mound entombs dozens of aristocrats and high functionaries.

I still would be unable to deny the circumstances of the stone's discovery in the vicinity of a large, circular ruin on the bottom of Rock Lake.

I hesitate to even begin to enumerate the paranormal incidents associated with it since my unconscious retrieval of the stone. After all, my intentions in documenting our efforts at Rock Lake did not include preternatural accounts. I sought only to straightforwardly present the story of a lost civilization as coherently and credibly as possible. All I feel qualified to report is that the stone seems special, even if it is finally confirmed as a natural simulacrum. Careful analysis is still underway to determine if the ship-like image is the result of coincidental natural forces or the handiwork of ancient man. In either case, we accept the stone as a gift from the water spirits to make us feel and think. We thank Diana Limnatis for her guidance in our quest and ask her blessing on Rock Lake.

·4·

Rock Lake's Enigmatic "Indian Shafts"

by Wayne N. May*

"Every mystery solved brings us closer to the threshold of a greater one."   *—Rachel Carson*

F all 1989 was supposed to be our last dive of the year at Rock Lake. On that cold, blustery Saturday in late October, author Frank Joseph, Professor of Civil Engineering James Scherz, and geologist Lloyd Hornbostel were exploring the north end for clues to the elusive pyramids

Wayne May is the publisher of Ancient American, *a popular science magazine that discusses evidence for overseas visitors to the Americas in pre-Columbian times. A resident of Lake Mills during the mid-1980s, Rock Lake was virtually in his backyard when he began his own hunt for the sunken pyramids. Mr. May played a prominent role in numerous lake expeditions, and continues to feature news about their current finds in his internationally known bimonthly periodical.*

down under the water. Meanwhile, master diver Doug Gossage, his Illinois assistant and I cruised our small vessel to the south end. We wanted to relocate a linear structure discovered earlier that summer. But the waves were rough and whitecaps reminding me of driven snow covered the lake.

Assigned to stay on board our three-man raft, my job was to hold the safety line steady when the two divers went below. Just as they disappeared over the side, the wind suddenly kicked up, pushing our raft away from their position, marked by bubbles rising to the surface from their regulators. Firmly rooted into place only a few minutes before, the anchor began dragging along the lake bottom. The force of the wind prevented me from staying in the divers' immediate vicinity. Against all my desperate efforts, the raft drifted helplessly in a south-southeasterly direction, heading toward Sandy Beach at the south end.

A depth finder was among the equipment. So, with nothing else to do, I switched it on just to watch the contours of the lake floor pass along far beneath the bottom of the raft. Suddenly, subsurface depths began dropping from thirty feet down to forty, fifty, sixty, even seventy feet. I was surprised, because standard fishing maps of the area showed little more than twenty feet of water here. I watched in fascination as rolling hills undulated across the bottom of the lake at depths of fifty and sixty feet. Clearly, the mapmakers were wrong.

Now depths began to abruptly climb back to thirty-foot levels. At twenty-nine feet, all readings suddenly dropped off into nothingness, then almost instantly returned to twenty-nine feet. Just then, the distinct image of a vertical shaft going straight down into the bottom of Rock Lake, its depth beyond measure, appeared across the screen. Moments later, a virtually identical target, but wider than the first one, came into view. Then a *third* shaft appeared, followed immediately by another. Were they lined up in single file? I was quick enough to photograph three of the four shafts, all of which had dropped to depths beyond the capabilities of the finder to determine. Thereafter, only the lake's smooth bottom slowly spread across the screen.

Recovering from my astonishment, I recalled reports of "Indian shafts" first glimpsed during the mid-1930s by free-divers from the University of Wisconsin swimming team engaged by historian Victor Taylor in his Rock Lake investigations. Just two years before my encounter with the shafts, Frank Joseph was boating in the same area when he went over the side. His anchor had refused to take hold of what he assumed (from the same inaccurate fisherman's maps) was a twenty-foot lake bottom. He followed the yellow line down to more than thirty feet, where he was surprised to see the anchor swaying free like a pendulum. Beneath him opened up a large hole about nine feet across.

Fortunately, a high, early afternoon sun shone almost directly down into the hole, providing unusually good clarity (about twenty-five feet visibility) throughout the yellowish green water. Joseph dove down into the shaft, its walls perfectly sheer. It seemed to him like a gigantic test tube thrust into the floor of the lake, because the lip of the hole was level with the lake bottom at thirty feet below the surface.

Sinking deeper into the shaft, he watched his depth gauge gradually drop from thirty to forty feet. Then down to fifty and sixty. Still, the bottom could not be seen. At seventy-six feet, Joseph finally reached the lowest part of the shaft. It gave every appearance of being man-made. Indeed, when we discussed these large holes with geologist Lloyd Hornbostel, he said he knew of no natural forces which could produce such perfectly formed features.

I believe the depression Frank Joseph explored was the sudden, seventy-plus-foot drop-off that appeared on the screen of our depth-finder just before the four narrower shafts were detected. They seem to have been only four to five feet in diameter. But their depth must have greatly exceeded the seventy-six feet indicated by our electronic instrument and earlier

Wayne May's photograph of sonar image of
an apparently bottomless pit in Rock Lake.

experienced by Joseph. In other words, the holes were too deep for the depth finder to determine.

Aware that the lake bottom is heavily silted, I wondered why the shafts were not filled in with organic debris. How deep are these apparently bottomless holes? And what are they? Were they subterranean silos used by the ancient inhabitants of Rock Lake when it was only a fraction of its present size? Are they prehistoric wells? Or do they represent something we cannot guess? They are certainly part of the mystery that pervades this strange place. Properly investigated, the Indian shafts may contribute importantly to a wider appreciation of the civilizers who, long ago, made Rock Lake their home.

.5.

Ancient Pyramids
or Glacial Debris?

*There are three steps in the revelation of any truth. In the first,
it is ridiculed. In the second, resisted. In the third, it is considered self-evident.*

—*Arthur Schopenhauer*

For all our usual lack of success in glimpsing one of the sunken structures, our hundreds of dives into Rock Lake provided us a thorough
acquaintance with the world beneath its surface. It proved to be an
unusual body of water, not at all like other glacier-formed lakes we knew.
Its floor is mostly a mud desert, but there are hills and gullies so subtly
molded into the underwater landscape that it is often difficult to distinguish them from the bottom itself. They could easily conceal a very large
structure from a diver already hindered by poor visibility.

There are also surprising, strange depressions were none ought to be.
Once while close to the western shore where the depth was no more than

seven or nine feet, we threw out the anchor, but for some reason it would not hold the bottom. I went over the side to investigate, following the twenty-foot line all the way to its end. I found the anchor swinging straight down on its nylon cord with the bottom far below. I descended to see how deep this unexpected area was and saw during my descent that I was entering a broad depression about fifty feet wide. My depth-gauge finally registered seventy-six feet. Above the depression, the water was no more than nine feet deep in the surrounding area. Such anomalies do not characterize lakes formed by glaciers.

Toward the north end of Rock Lake, near the middle, where depths range from thirty to forty feet, a ridge rises up suddenly to only fourteen feet beneath the surface. Known as "the drop-off," its western slope plunges at a steep angle to more than ninety feet, the lake's deepest section. Rock Lake actually resembles two different bodies of water below the surface. While the southern half is entirely muddy, the northern is as rocky in many parts as a stone quarry.

When I visited Slovenia in 1990, I stayed near Lake Bled, unquestionably glacier-formed and typical of its kind. Other than having a comparable size, its resemblance to Rock Lake was negligible. The Balkan lake is round, slightly ovoid, nearly three times as deep and with a subsurface resembling a teacup filled with impenetrably turbid water. It is devoid of stones and is as unlike Rock Lake as any other body of water on earth. Bledsko Jezero, as it is known to the Slovenes, is the classic Ice Age lake, yet it shares virtually nothing in common with Wisconsin's Rock Lake, which was supposedly formed entirely by an identical natural process.

Despite its decidedly unglacial appearance, when academics finally broke their long silence on the possibility of sunken, man-made formations, they opined that whatever might lie on the bottom of Rock Lake was certainly the result of the glacier that created it ten thousand years ago.

"People have been searching for pyramids in that lake forever," said Lynne Goldstein, professor of anthropology at the University of Wisconsin, Madison. "Although there is something down there with a pyramidal shape, from all the data I've seen, it appears to be a natural formation."[1] With Dr. Goldstein began a general acceptance among her colleagues that the subsurface formations were actually nothing more than glacial debris. As the glacier that carved out Rock Lake retreated, it left behind mounds of material mistaken by observers for man-made objects. Such naturally formed piles are known as *drumlins* and *kames.*

However, the glacial deposit theory begins to disintegrate with the very definition of these terms. A drumlin is an oval-shaped hill or a long, trailing ridge of variously mixed rocks and matter, neither of which matches any of the descriptions of the sunken structures. Kames are likewise steep hills or ridges composed of gravel or sand deposited in contact with glacial ice. No one has ever claimed to have seen anything resembling a kame on the bottom of Rock Lake. Moreover, if the structures in question were glacially formed, then Rock Lake is a geologic freak, a special rarity, because neither drumlins nor kames are known to occupy the bottom of any other lake on earth. If the stones John Kennedy retrieved from one of the structures belonged to a drumlin, they should have been scarred from glacial action, tumbling them together into a heap. Instead, they were easily identified as quartzite from a riverbed. They showed unmistakable signs of long-term water erosion, not glacial action. And no glacier could have created the volcano- or donut-shaped stone mounds, with their precisely circular craters, seen by numerous divers in Rock Lake.

Despite these elementary observations, Goldstein's glacial deposit theory appears to have become the official explanation within a scientific establishment that disdains the fantastic claims of mere amateurs. R. Birmingham, Wisconsin's state archaeologist, and Thomas Kehoe, curator of anthropology at the Milwaukee Public Museum, agreed with her that the Rock Lake anomalies are only glacial debris. Remarkably, the real difference between those who believe the structures are man-made and those convinced they are not is that the believers are mostly divers who have, collectively, devoted hundreds of hours of bottom-time to the lake, while the nonbelievers are largely professional theorists who have never gone near the water. As Richard Bennett, owner of a Wisconsin diving academy, said in 1986, "I think I've spent enough time underwater to know what's natural and what isn't. I believe those pyramids are not of natural origin."[2]

Professional astronomers gratefully acknowledge the observations of responsible amateurs. Not so most professional archaeologists and anthropologists. The tragedy lies not only in the gap here between the academics and the public, nor in the important discoveries lost or, at least, sidetracked until rediscovered later, but the physical danger of obliteration of unacknowledged sites of unrecognized value. As Dr. Scherz concluded in his report on Rock Lake's first sonar survey, "The underwater features should be protected from destruction by trophy-hunting divers until they are at least thoroughly studied. If there is a high probability that they are man-made artifacts themselves, then their future protection should likewise be assured."[3] That very succinctly sums up the chief motivation of everyone who has come to accept the underwater site at Rock Lake for what is really is; namely, a forgotten American civilization's City of the Dead that must be preserved against damage and destruction.

So long as most scientific officials refuse to take the matter seriously, the sunken structures will remain vulnerable to the ravages of irresponsible treasure hunters. We recall with deep-felt regret the plundering of Aztalan's pyramids in the last century and the wholesale obliteration of the dozens of effigy mounds that lined the shores of Rock Lake until the 1920s. If in the future the underwater monuments are finally and officially recognized for their human authenticity after they have been damaged or destroyed, the world will know who to blame.

•6•

The Evidence
Speaks for Itself

Man does not have the only memory. The earth remembers. The stones remember. If you know how to listen, they will tell you many things.

—*Claude Kuwanijuma*
Hopi spiritual leader

Max Nohl's description of the conical pyramid he discovered under Rock Lake in 1937 included a cement-like substance that clung to portions of the structure. In 1988, Doug Gossage reported finding similar material on a pyramidal mound in the northeastern quadrant.

The following year, he was actually able to retrieve fragments of the brittle compound from the Limnatis structure. They were taken to Dr. Martin Flowers, professor of geology at the University of Chicago's mineralogical department. His examination showed that the whitish coating covering a broad section of the structure's western wall was a calcite based plaster made by crushing mollusk shells and other calcareous material into a fine powder, then mixing it with water to form a thick plaster that hardened as it dried.[1] Obviously, the process could not have been accomplished underwater through some natural agency. It was a man-made plaster, not marl, a naturally occurring mixture of clayey limestone. Similar tests at the University of Wisconsin in Madison contradicted Flowers' findings, but samples analyzed there may not have belonged to the same material he studied.

But outside evidence points to human manufacture of the apparent "cement" taken from the sunken structure. The walls of nearby Aztalan were originally coated entirely by the same substance that clings to the Limnatis pyramid. The Aztalan stockade was plastered over to give it a smooth finish. Precisely the same technique and material were used to coat the far more extensive stockade walls of Cahokia, a Mississippian ceremonial center of grandiose proportions that flourished a thousand years ago in Illinois, and again at the walls of another ancient city contemporary with and closely resembling Aztalan in southern Indiana, Angel Mounds. Sixty-five miles northeast of Angel Mounds lie the Wyandotte Caves, where hundreds of tons of dry limestone were mined by an unknown race over the course of centuries. The calcareous material was used in the production of the whitish plaster found at Angel Mounds, Cahokia, Aztalan, and under Rock Lake, all within the continuity of Mississippian culture.

Actually, three different kinds of cement have been found on underwater features in Tyranena's depths. The darker gray material is heavier and less brittle than its whiter counterpart; the latter has been seen less often beneath the external surfaces of the structures and may have been used to bond the stones into position. The thinner, more plaster-like substance was probably employed as a decorative coating to give the monument a smooth, external finish, the same ornamental dressing on the walls (and even on many of the private dwellings and public temples) at Angel Mounds, Cahokia,

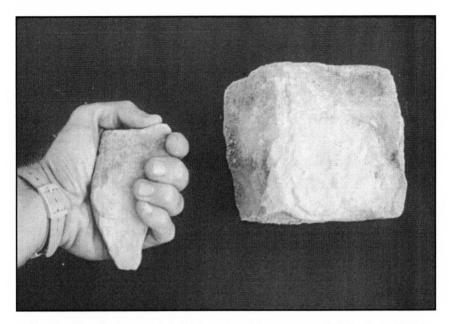

At right, a verified man-made brick retrieved from a stone circle in the southeast quadrant of Rock Lake. The hand-held stone may be a tool for pounding, but laboratory testing at Wisconsin's Beloit College testing was inconclusive.

and Aztalan. These two kinds of cement found in Rock Lake might be explained by an alternate source for the material. Salts Cave, part of Kentucky's Mammoth Cave Park, was mined anciently for gypsum, from which a white plaster was known to have been manufactured. Preserved human fecal droppings in the cave revealed that the miners ate cultivated foods identical to the specialized crops harvested by the original inhabitants of Aztalan and did not belong to the hunter-gatherer tribes of the region. Apparently, the Rock Lake inhabitants felt that gypsum was valuable enough to import it from Salts Cave, more than five hundred miles away. Perhaps they even worked the gypsum mines themselves.

While all the evidence suggests the cone-shaped pyramids were constructed as free-standing stone structures only occasionally bonded internally with the heavier, dark gray adhesive, at least some of the larger, tent-shaped mounds were completely coated in the limestone-mix plaster. In their original condition, their walls would have appeared smoothly covered, just as the stockades of Aztalan, and so on, presented a flat surface over the posts covered by the plaster. The Aztalaners' preference for covering their foremost monuments was extended to their temple-mounds, which were originally encased in clay caps to give the structures a smooth appearance, the same cultural trait recurring on the buildings under Rock Lake. It seems clear, then, that the limestone material retrieved by divers from the subsurface targets is man-made and part of the identical cultural forces prehistorically at work throughout southern Wisconsin and the rest of America's ancient Midwest.

Yet a third kind of bonding material encountered on some of the linear stone mounds under Rock Lake is a smooth, medium gray, cement-like substance with surprising traces of iron. Divers who retrieved samples for Dr. Robert Salzer's office at Beloit College reported that the cement covered very broad sections of a sunken ridge-top pyramid. Analysis revealed that the structures in question were once covered by a cap of mixed clay and earth that had not been washed away by water. Instead, it hardened over time into a material resembling smooth adhesive.

Here seemed positive proof that the linear features were man-made ridge-top mounds after all, because the same construction technique compared exactly with some of Aztalan's monuments, such as the Greenwood Group: stone chambers covered by mounds of earth.

But in a letter I received from Dr. Salzer (January 8, 1992), he wrote, "My impression is that the (apparently) unsorted gravel/pebble/cobble 'stuff' is held together by reddish brown sand; the color being a function of the presence of what is probably iron-rich minerals. Thanks to ancient glacial activity, such iron minerals are regularly present in the soils of southeastern Wisconsin. While excavating in northern Wisconsin some years ago, I encountered instances where reddish brown sands had been cemented

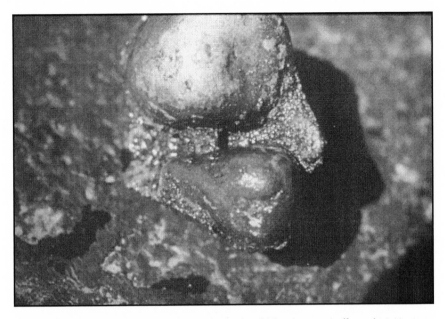

Proof of the Rock Lake structure's artificial identity: A small specimen removed from the western flank of the Limnatis stone mound. According to geologist Dr. Martin Flowers (University of Chicago), the two rocks are bonded by a man-made material, probably pulverized mollusk shells combined with water and clay to create a primitive cement.

together and I believe that soil-scientists and sedimentologists refer to this (wholly natural phenomenon) as gleying. This apparently occurs when soils/sediments are subjected to long periods of water-logged conditions. It is possible that what you have is an example of such consolidated sediments. One thing seems clear to me: I would expect that any man-made 'plaster' or 'cement' would contain carbonates in some form or another, and I do not believe that such carbonates are present."

Later, in a telephone conversation, Dr. Salzer conceded that "gleying" might have been produced if the structures on which the process appears were originally covered with earth, as were the stone chambers of Aztalan's Greenwood mounds. For example, were Aztalan's Pyramid of the Sun submerged underwater for many centuries, its exterior, too, could harden into a gley. It appears, then, that this third kind of suspected cement is not some anciently artificial adhesive, although it may be the natural result of a man-made coating of earth that originally capped the elongated pyramids before they were drowned. This interpretation is lent some credence by the fact that in all the bottom-time divers have devoted to exploring Rock Lake since 1937, they have never encountered anything even faintly resembling gley, except on the pyramidal structures.

Less equivocal evidence of human activity at the bottom of Rock Lake comprises the drowned effigies in its eastern quadrant. The turtle and head-less-man mounds found by our side-scan sonar were certainly among the most thrilling discoveries ever made in that mysterious body of water. They constitute exciting proof that remnants of a lost culture do indeed exist on the murky floor. Both are lent splendid authenticity by parallel effigies found on nearby dry land. Outside the walls of Aztalan itself, an archaeological dig unearthed the ritual burial of a tall man, since referred to as the Giant, who had been interred in a tomb still containing all the marks of respect—sim-ple grave goods—but curiously minus a head. Close by, in Jefferson County, another headless giant was surveyed in the late nineteenth century before its unfortunate obliteration under the plow. The mound was seventy-nine feet long and represented a decapitated man.[2] Clearly, ritual beheading at Rock Lake-Aztalan belonged to some important cult practice observed by the ancient inhabitants. That Jefferson County's headless-giant mound was part of the ceremonial life of the Rock Lake area seems clear, if only because it was unique among the more than ten thousand effigies that once spread so magnificently across the Wisconsin landscape.

A study of the side-scan map revealed yet another strange feature dis-played by the Rock Lake effigy mounds. About 350 feet from them, oppo-site the shore toward the swimming area, the sonar identified a low circle on the mud bottom. I recognized it at once from its location as the same heap of stones from which I retrieved a brick qualified as "man-made" by

Diver Jason Bucholtz holds a deer bone he retrieved from one of the stone monuments of Rock Lake. The bone is cracked to extract its marrow, a delicacy relished by the ancient Aztalaners.

Dr. Salzer in 1988. Investigators knew then that the supposed "rock pile" was in fact the collapsed remains of a cone-shaped structure. Our subsurface map showed that this ruined pyramid was oriented due west on a straight alignment with the headless man mound. From this conical monument an observer would have seen the sun set over the headless man, the turtle or through the gap between them on special days of the year, when the area was still dry land. The orientation of the effigies to the circular monument is beyond question and constitutes another marvelous piece of valid evidence authenticating the man-made origins of Rock Lake's underwater objects.

Reaffirming that authenticity is the symbolic inter-relationship of the three figures: Sunset on the emblems of death (the headless man) and transcendence (the turtle), with a magical period in between them both when they are suspended in a twilight balance. The esoteric imagery that once functioned at what has long since become Rock Lake must have been of a dramatic and uplifting nature. Moreover, the effigy mounds' alignments to the conical pyramid belong to the same cosmic concepts similarly in use among the complimentary astronomical fixes of nearby Aztalan. That ceremonial center's skeleton without a skull most likely belonged to the central player in one of these religious dramas.

The headless man's companion mound was no less enlightening about ancient Tyranena. Alone, the turtle signifies the ability to survive both on land and in the water. It also represents coming ashore, implying arrival by sea. Numerous traditions of Native American peoples, including the Ho Chunk, who once occupied the Jefferson County area, claim their ancestors came to North America, referred to as "Turtle Island" (!), after the Great Flood destroyed their former world. The name "Turtle Island" describes this ancestral arrival over the waters by boat, just as the turtle wades ashore wearing its shell.

The turtle- and man-mounds in Rock Lake are the same size and placed side by side. Their juxtaposition is intentional and may have been part of a turtle-cult of the dead. Given Rock Lake's identity as a necropolis, the western orientation of the two mounds and the turtle shell excavated from Aztalan's ritual grave site seem appropriate. Indeed, as mentioned earlier, the turtle makes a perfect transformational creature, as it "crosses over" from one dimension into another, just as the human soul passes from earthly existence through the waters of death.

While all the bones found thus far have been traced to deer, a specimen of human remains was recovered from Rock Lake as recently as 1982, when the large hank of a man's scalp was pulled into the boat of a surprised fisherman, who immediately notified the police. Divers from the Lake Mills Fire Department scoured the waters in which it was hauled out for three days, interrupted only by nightfall, but encountered no trace of the body they expected to find. There were no reports of lake accidents or missing persons, and the authorities chalked up the discovery to yet another mystery of their mysterious lake. But ever since, thoughtful pyramid-hunters have wondered if the scalp in fact belonged to a body of one of the ancient dead reposing in a stone monument that had been sufficiently ruined by time for a fisherman's hook to catch on the exposed corpse still otherwise preserved in Rock Lake's icy waters. Or perhaps it was a trophy buried as a grave good along with the deceased and accidentally snagged by the fisherman. Wisconsin's aboriginals were known, after all, to take scalps as honorable prizes in war. For investigators aware of the abundant evidence supporting the lake as an ancient necropolis, the scalp retrieved from its waters underscores their conclusions.

But the evidence most sought after has proved the most elusive. Out of all the many hundreds (at least) of photographs taken above and below Rock Lake, only a tiny handful document the objects observed since the turn of the century. Given the extremely difficult conditions in this moody body of water, lack of success is not surprising. Numerous interacting factors of currents, varying temperatures, lighting, algae bloom, the ever-present silt, wave action, boat traffic, wind, rain, even passing clouds, all conspire to frustrate the most persistent photographer. In a word, Rock Lake is uncooperative. Its typically optimum visibility of ten feet simply does not allow a camera to be pulled back far enough to take in a structure in its entirety, resulting in photographs that show only fields of rock. Doug Gossage's videotape of the Limnatis feature somewhat overcame this restriction. He kept the camera rolling as he swam along the full length of the target, providing the viewer with an improved conception of its pyramidal configuration. Subsurface photography of large objects with corners and massive bulk are particularly difficult subjects, because of the distortion factor that naturally occurs in water. Contrasts are lost and depth of field flattens out. Lenses exist to somewhat correct these handicaps, but they are costly and not always effective. As fate would have it, the finest aerial photographs of the Great Triangle in the southern half of Rock Lake were destroyed by fire. Steve Dempsey's color slides, which were featured at a meeting of Lake Mills Ancient Earthworks Society in the late 1980s, clearly showed the precise outlines of the monumental figure beneath the surface. The loss of these superb photographs is still keenly felt.

Underwater artificial lights are worse than useless, because their radiance reflects back from all the detritus hanging suspended in the water. Photographs in Rock Lake and over it are entirely matters of thorough, advanced preparation, superhuman patience and, most importantly, luck. Only into my fifth year of investigation were the gods kind enough to part the veils and allow us to take a few relatively clear photographs that show the structures in all their man-made magnificence.

But more significant evidence is available among the many eyewitnesses to Rock Lake's subsurface anomalies. The people who claim to have seen its lost pyramids are not a collection of crackpots and overheated enthusiasts. They include diving instructors, surveyors, teachers, university professors, salvage operators, newspaper photographers, doctors—persons whose livelihood depends on their training and expertise as professional observers. It is difficult to dismiss the observations of Max Nohl, inventor of the scuba, holder of world diving records and scientific pioneer in underwater technology. That three generations of highly qualified and reliable persons have encountered the sunken structures should give even the severest critic pause. If the question of Rock Lake's mystery were tested in a court of law, the men and women who could testify on its behalf would make star witnesses.

In addition to their number are the many not so highly trained, but nonetheless intelligent and honest individuals, whose desire to learn the truth is no less a motivation of their quest. All of them have acted with a consistent sense of responsibility, a high standard of behavior that has enabled many years of research to continue without injury or mishap to anyone. Such a record of safety and hard work does not bespeak clowns playing at archae-ology, but rather typifies serious investigators who want to uncover the lost history of their country. Their observations weigh just as significantly in the balance of opinion as the most convincing material evidence.

.7.

What Are the Pyramids and How Were They Made?

Make not that impossible which seems unlikely.

—Shakespeare
Measure for Measure

The stone formations at the bottom of Rock Lake as much resemble the temple-mounds of Aztalan as they do those of the earlier, although closely related ceremonial center at Cahokia, some three hundred miles away, and another Mississippian site in Wisconsin. Northwest of the Aztalan enclosure, a row of dome-shaped earthen mounds on the top of a rise running north to south finds a very close parallel in the group of stone "chimneys" of approximate if not equal dimensions atop a former stream bank, likewise in a north-south line, in a central section of the lake. Referred to as the Greenwood Group, the Aztalan domes enclose cone-shaped stone pyramids.

Mentioned in chapter 3 was the discovery on November 3, 1990, of an underwater volcano-like configuration identical, save only for its stone construction, to ancient earth-graves in Dunn County, Wisconsin. Other sunken structures are duplicated in Cahokia's mounds. The colossal tent-shaped features in Rock Lake, such as the Limnatis, are known as "ridge top" figures at the Illinois site. Conical mounds may be seen there as well, together with the so-called "bread loaf" type encountered less frequently in the lake. Excavations at Cahokia revealed the three classes of mounds found identically under Rock Lake were sepulchers reflecting the status of the individuals they contained. Conical burials held a single body or a group of only four or five persons and are assumed to have belonged exclusively to men and families of special importance. Perhaps they were outstanding warriors or shamans.

The long, ridge-top mounds were reserved for rulers, certainly the most powerful personages in society, because their contents revealed elaborate burials of mica flakes imported from New England, sheets of copper from Michigan, abundant shells from the Gulf of Mexico and hundreds of sacrificed maidens. Here too is valid comparison with the Rock Lake discovery made by Michael Kutska's divers, when they found a cache of shells in a ridge-top structure. The "bread loaf" structures were ossuaries, reliquaries for thousands of mixed human bones, all belonging to the aristocrats who served the ruler and organized the lower orders of their society.

Construction practices were similarly applied to the three types. Pits were dug for the deceased, then covered over with a heap of earth which was worked into the desired configuration and raised in several alternating levels of internally reinforcing clay to hold the structure's shape. Sometimes mounds were begun before burial, and bodies were placed on the first layer or tier, upon which the monument was completed.

The features on the bottom of Rock Lake correspond to the Cahokia mounds, differing only in the materials used. Graves were dug for the dead

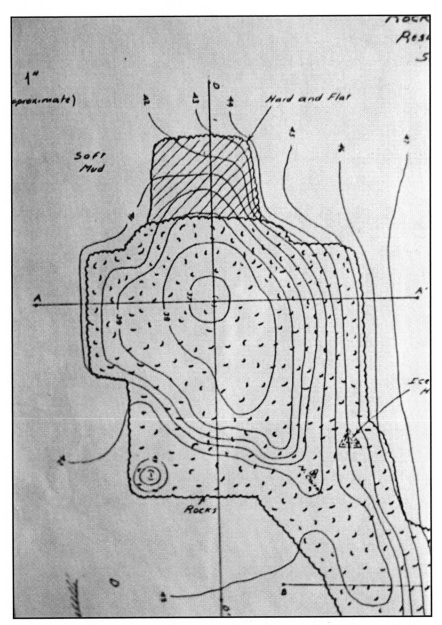

Sonar image of the north end of the Limnatis stone mound
reveals its angular, obviously man-made configuration.
The feature connecting it at the top appears to be a ramp.

on the shores of the former lake level and along the banks of the streams which drained into it. Stones transported from the nearby river due north of the site were heaped up over the burial to form a ridge-top, bread loaf or conical design, and bonded by a calcium carbonate adhesive.

Wayne May speculates that the glacial debris deposited in the north end of the lake was used as construction material by the ancient pyramid builders, who regarded it as a natural quarry close at hand. In any case, the monuments are solid structures with no internal chambers, save the shallow pits on which they sit, although some burials may have been laid out on the lower platforms of unfinished tombs, which were subsequently completed on top of earlier graves, as funeral architects did in Cahokia. Finally, the full length of the pyramid's exterior was coated with a limestone or gypsum-base plaster that gave the structure a smooth, white appearance. Not all the features were so coated, however, and none of the conical mounds show evidence of a decorative finish, although it may have dissolved or disintegrated over the centuries.

But similarities between Cahokia and Rock Lake do not end in a comparison of building styles. Just as the Limnatis and its companion structures were built on the shore of the original glacier lake, so the leading conical and ridge-top mounds in Cahokia's central plaza stood on the shore of what was formerly an artificial tarn, a sacred lake.

Aztalan itself suggests how the inverted, ice-cream-cone-like pyramids standing on the floor of Rock Lake were made. Some of the mounds in the Greenwood Group overlooking the walled enclosure contained stone cones. Their builders began by laying out an unmortared circle of stones, piling them on top of each other. As the levels ascended at an inclined angle, a corresponding strata of earth rose as a platform on which the builders stood until the top of the stone pyramid was completed. It would have been hidden inside the surrounding dome of earth, in which its function was to securely hold the astronomical alignment post that projected from the top of the mound.

This Aztalan parallel may explain why some of the "chimneys" at the bottom of Rock Lake appear to be made of nothing more than stones piled up on top of each other into the shape of an inverted cone without any sign of a bonding substance. Perhaps, like their Greenwood counterparts, they were originally used to stabilize alignment posts inside earthen mounds long since washed away by the water, leaving their conical stone cores as nothing more than free-standing piles. Their unmortared condition might explain the circular heaps of like stone, giving the appearance of a collapsed building, found on the lake bottom. Some, at least, were unable to stand and did indeed fall in on themselves. Moreover, a few of the "chimney" types discovered in 1991 did not rise to a pointed apex. Their tops were open and hollow, as were the Greenwood Group mounds. Perhaps these Rock Lake cones were likewise the stabilizing mounts for astronomical fixes, when they stood on dry land many centuries ago.

Resemblances between the structures under Rock Lake and those at other ancient sites in the Midwest make a persuasive argument on behalf of the authenticity of the sunken monuments. And although there are no plans to excavate them, their close correspondence to the funeral architecture of Cahokia, Aztalan and Dunn County clearly identifies the underwater features as tombs. Doubtless, their many hundreds of tons of stone still conceal the remains of the men who organized, administered and led Wisconsin's forgotten civilization.

·8·

How Did the
Pyramids Sink?

We all agree that your theory is mad. The problem that divides
us is this: Is it sufficiently crazy to be right?

—*Niels Bohr*

ince they were first glimpsed from Claude and Lee Wilson's boat at
the turn of the century, several theories have been advanced to explain
how pyramids got to the bottom of Rock Lake. An early explanation
had Paleo-Indians rafting tons of stones out onto the lake, into which they
were dumped through a kind of funnel or chute made of bark to distribute
the stones in a roughly pyramidal configuration.[1] Why anyone would have
gone to such trouble was not explained by the proponents of this theory.

Victor Taylor, the schoolteacher who organized the first serious inquiry
of the structures in 1935, learned through his research that a prolonged
drought took place in southern Wisconsin coincidental with the last days of
Aztalan. Now known as the Little Ice Age, the first half of the fourteenth

century witnessed an extended period of cold, dry air that prevented rainfall, perhaps for several years. Taylor speculated that the lake dropped far below its normal levels at this time, practically drying up, until rocky debris from the glacier that formed it nine thousand years before was exposed. With these stones, the ancient inhabitants built pyramidal formations to flatter their gods in an effort to regain divine favor and call back the life-giving rains. In subsequent years, the lake rose to its former levels, submerging the structures.

Dendrochronology, or the dating of past events as revealed by tree ring patterns, confirms that an important drought took place in the Lake Mills area around the time Aztalan was evacuated.[2] While lake levels must have been affected by prolonged rainless conditions, and at least some of the structures which today lie twelve to eighteen feet beneath the surface may have been exposed, it seems unlikely that the levels were low enough to allow the construction of the Limnatis, the Kennedy and other features presently under more than sixty feet of water. Seven hundred years ago, Rock Lake could have been fifteen feet lower than it is today. But given even the consequences of an exceptionally long drought, the stone structures would still lie at least thirty to forty feet beneath the surface. Moreover, Rock Lake is spring fed and less dependent on rainfall for its existence.

Our side-scan sonar surveys clearly showed several previous lake levels going back 3,500 years, and along the oldest of these, on what had been the shoreline, were found virtually all of the stone structures. It would appear, then, that they were built at a time when the lake was substantially lower than its present level, in an era that preceded by many centuries the beginning of Aztalan, in the early twelfth century. In order for them to have been built in their deep water location, they must have been constructed when Rock Lake was only a fraction of its present size, three and a half millennia ago. In all that time, the natural springs may have been sufficient to expand the lake and raise its water level, but their output, unless drastically greater in the ancient past, would have been wholly unable to enlarge little more than a pond about 350 feet long, 120 feet across, and perhaps 30 feet deep into a lake two and a half miles wide and ninety feet at its deepest point.

There is yet a more dramatic explanation for the existence of the stone monuments sixty feet down: They were deliberately sunk. For evidence, investigators cite a large, deep riverbed lying only three hundred feet north of Rock Lake. Many centuries ago, it fed a tributary to the Crawfish River that still flows through Aztalan. A scenario for what took place begins with the ancient civilizers erecting stone temples and tombs along the shores of the tiny glacier lake and on the banks of its streams. As their culture began to fall, perhaps to hostile elements within society or invaders from without, or because the copper trade collapsed, they sought to protect their sacred burial grounds from profanation. They excavated a canal from the powerful river lying due north, directing its waters into the holy precinct and inundating all its shrines and tombs underwater that grew to become Rock Lake.

Any trace of the canal that caused the flood was obliterated when the modern beach and road were installed. But the dry river bed is still clearly discernible. Excavating the necessary canal by no means lay beyond the technical abilities of the ancient inhabitants. They were known to have completed serious irrigation projects, the most notable being a stone aqueduct that extended from the northern end of Aztalan, perhaps to Rock Lake itself, three miles away. A canal only three hundred feet long would certainly have presented far less of an engineering challenge. The ancient engineers may have even controlled lake levels with their canal in order to perform the walk-on-water trick described in Ho Chunk tradition. Perhaps they allowed the water to just cover the tops of the larger, deeper structures, over which the torch-bearing shamans paraded to the stone monuments on higher ground, where they appeared as islets or to float on the water. After the shamans' civilization declined, the canal was neglected and the river eventually broke through its sluices to inundate the remainder of the lake.

Substantiation for the flood theory rests largely, although not entirely, in persistent Native American tradition. The Menomonie, whose connections with Rock Lake through the ancient copper trade was certain, believe that underworld spirits caused a frightful deluge, after which they went to dwell forever at the bottom of a sacred lake.[3] The Yaqui Indians claim the cone-shaped pyramids at the bottom of Rock Lake were shrines, whose apexes were intentionally broken off to deconsecrate them before they were flooded under water to protect them from blasphemers.

A particularly unusual find was made by divers working on leads supplied by the side-scan sonar, in the summer of 1990, when they discovered an earthquake fault line running north and south, a quarter of a mile from the northern shore. Speculation at once arose that some seismic violence may have broken open a passage from the river running north of the site into the little glacial valley to abruptly inundate the sacred area with a cataclysmic flood. I smiled to think that my own search for Atlantis had brought me to an Atlantean apocalypse in Wisconsin. But there was no way to determine the age of the Rock Lake fault, which might predate human occupation of the area by many thousands of years. There was not enough evidence to positively connect the submarine earthquake fault line with a possible flood that resulted in Rock Lake.

In any case, the lake rose altogether by a remarkable sixty feet after 1500 B.C., and even though man-made dams beginning in the 1830s raised levels from seven to twenty feet, it is difficult to account for some natural occurrence that could have dumped at least another forty feet of water into the lake in only three thousand years. Also, the notion of lake levels controlled by ancient chiefs to overawe and thereby manipulate their subservient classes coincides with known cultural patterns at Aztalan. There, its Pyramid of the Sun, in the keeping of ruling aristocrats, similarly impressed the laboring masses of farmers, hunters and artisans by predicting significant celestial phenomena. It is nonetheless thrilling to wonder if the stone temples and tombs lying on the bottom of Rock Lake were long ago intentionally flooded by a man-made deluge to save them from desecration or use them as part of a magical drama to enthrall their people.

Logically, such a flood must have taken place either through human engineering or natural (seismic) forces, because nothing else can explain the forty- to fifty-foot increase in the level of Rock Lake after 1500 B.C. Either through the intentions of man or the will of nature, Wisconsin does indeed have its own Atlantis.

.9.

How Old Are the Pyramids?

When the academic experts state that something is possible, they are probably right. When they state that something is impossible, they are probably wrong.

—*Arthur C. Clarke*

Until the *Sea Search* finished her sweep of the bottom of Rock Lake, the structures there defied all attempts to date them. It was generally assumed, however, that Victor Taylor had been correct when he determined that they were built as a religious response to the Little Ice Age drought of the early 1300s. But when the prehistoric lake levels were defined for the first time by the side-scan sonar, Dr. Scherz reported that the former shoreline on which Bass Rock Bar, Limnatis, Kennedy and several of the larger, deeper structures rested, represented the actual limits of the lake around 1500 B.C.! The date came as a total shock to all investigators and seemed to take Tyranena in a single stroke completely out of Aztalan's cultural orbit.

Yet, this period fits in perfectly with Aztalan's *raison d'etat* as a copper-mining town. Michigan's mines in the Upper Peninsula were primarily worked from 3000 to 1200 B.C., so the society that built Rock Lake's sunken necropolis flourished at the same time the copper trade was booming. Rock Lake was probably an early way station centrally located for shippers of that trade during voyages from Michigan to the Mississippi. Tyranena's position just below the heavy-snow line made it a natural and ideal stopover or clearing-house for the cargoes of raw minerals and their handlers. The site presently under sixty feet of water must have been occupied before 1500 B.C., because such large structures are the products of a prosperous, populous society, which developed out of the rich copper trade over eighteen centuries. Settlement in such a fortuitous location was wonderfully situated for the accumulation of wealth. It may have collapsed only when the copper mines were suddenly abandoned in 1200 B.C.

The earliest reliable date for Aztalan is around A.D. 1100. The enormous gap in time between events in Rock Lake and the first known settlement of Aztalan in the first decades of the twelfth century undoubtedly results from insufficient excavation. Only a fraction of the enclosure and its immediate environs were researched and all studies have been confined to its later phases. More extensive and deeper subsoil investigations could push occupation periods further back in time. Despite the two millennia separating Aztalan's earliest known dates from Tyranena, the Rock Lake precinct, even in ruins and partially or even completely submerged, must have been well known for centuries after its abandonment throughout ancient Mid-America, as much for its unique setting as for the sanctity of its tombs, otherwise the Aztalaners would not have chosen the Rock Lake area in which to settle.

If Tyranena was the beginning of civilization in prehistoric Wisconsin, Aztalan was its end. Everything that came in between is unknown. The stone structures today nearest the surface may have been raised, or in any case used, by twelfth-century builders from nearby Aztalan when lake levels were much lower than at present. There is no doubt, however, that the much larger monuments now lying sixty feet down stood along the former shoreline, gleaming in the sunshine of thirty-five centuries ago.

·10·

Native Americans Remember the Pyramid Drama

*Even the rocks which seem to be dumb, as they swelter in the
sun along the silent shore, thrill with memories of stirring events
connected with the lives of my people.*

—*Chief Seattle, 1854*

Ho Chunk ("Winnebago") Indians resided in the Lake Mills area
when the first white settlers arrived during the early 1830s. The
Ho-Chun-Ga-Ra, or "Fish Eaters," as they sometimes referred to
themselves, preceded the European newcomers by perhaps two centuries,
but numerous other tribes wandered back and forth across southern Wisconsin long before them. The earliest known inhabitants of the area were
the Mandans, among the most interesting and skilled of all the indigenous

peoples. They, too, erected stockaded walls, although not so extensive or magnificent as Aztalan's ramparts, and preserved intriguing traditions of ancestral arrivals from a Great Flood.[1]

But the Mandans were builders of neither the underwater necropolis of Rock Lake nor the ceremonial enclosure of Aztalan. Of Siouan stock, the Ho Chunk maintained an oral heritage of all those tribes who came before them in a special body of folk memories called the Worak, recited histories of the region. It was distinct from the Wykuh, which dealt with religious and nature tales, recounted only in wintertime.

The Worak was not a collection of fables, but the veritable tribal memory of past events, sometimes stretching back many generations. Primitive societies are generally ultraconservative in the preservation of their folklore, as exampled by Homer's *Iliad,* an oral tradition of events separated by at least four hundred years from the bard. The Native American memory of Rock Lake and Aztalan was enshrined in the Worak, which the Ho Chunk were willing to share with the whites until too many greedy individuals, hearing of the ancient civilizers, dug up Aztalan's mounds in search of nonexistent treasure. The Ho Chunk henceforward kept the Worak to themselves, save for the rare confidence of a tribal elder in a trustworthy white man.

When the first European settlers reached the shores of Rock Lake in the 1830s, they saw several little islands all surmounted by curious stone buildings. These were the "rock tepees" the Ho Chunk said belonged originally to the "old foreign chiefs." They were a tribe of powerful sorcerers, who allowed no one near the lake except on special occasions. Then everybody had to attend magical ceremonies down by the shore, always at night, when the moon and stars were worshiped as gods. To demonstrate the particular favor that was given to them by heaven, the ancient shamans paraded out across the face of the waters with blazing torches outstretched in both hands. They walked to the sacred islands which supported the temples and shrines of their most honored dead. But their procession across the lake was a trick, because only they knew the exact positions of stone causeways lying just beneath the surface.

According to Dr. James Scherz, the Menomonie have known for unknown centuries about the conical mounds at the bottom of Rock Lake. Tribal elders, the record keepers of their nation, say that at least some of the submerged monuments are the same as northern Michigan's pokasawa pits, rough stone towers resembling firebreaks, but of a spiritual significance the Menomonie are still reluctant to share with outsiders. This Native American tradition is in itself a wonderful proof for the existence of the controversial structures.

In 1990, Dr. Scherz was able to speak with a tribal elder and keeper of the Worak, who was quite literally on his deathbed. He told Dr. Scherz, who had won the old man's respect and confidence, that the large structure lying in the deeper part of Rock Lake was indeed a place of ancient worship once revered as the Temple of the Moon Goddess, to whom the whole lake had been consecrated. The known lunar aspects of the site confirm the elder's tradition. Just north of Rock Lake, a farmer plowing his field in the dried riverbed uncovered a smooth, round stone decorated with tiny crescent moons. Remarkably, an identical stone was later discovered at the south end of the lake. Not far from the southeast shore, someone found a crescent moon masterfully carved from a single piece of obsidian.

Then there is the northern orientation of the Limnatis Temple of the Moon Goddess, an orientation associated with the lowest lunar rising at other prehistoric ceremonial centers in North America, such as Ohio's Octagon Mound. We recall, too, the celestial alignments discovered (again by Dr. Scherz) at the temple-mounds of Aztalan, astronomical coordinates which compliment Ho Chunk descriptions of moon and star worship at Rock Lake.

·11·

The Monster of Rock Lake

According to Algonkin legends, the great serpent always came up the Mississippi searching for copper, for which it had an enormous appetite.

—*L. Taylor Hansen*

As though the stories of ancient pyramids at the bottom of Rock Lake were not controversial enough, belief in a monster prowling its depths is at least as venerable as stories of the sunken monuments. As we shall learn, however, both legends are connected in Native American folklore, although accounts of modern sightings of the creature fall somewhere between the actual and the psychological, some might say the paranormal.

An early recorded encounter with the monster took place in the summer of 1887, as two middle-aged fishermen rowed their boat across the tranquil waters of Rock Lake. Edward McKenzie and D. W. Seybert were boyhood friends who had grown up together in Lake Mills, then only a very small town. The fish were not biting that Sunday afternoon, at least in the middle of the lake, so McKenzie and Seybert rowed toward the first sand bar at the swampy southwest end, where they hoped for better prospects. Maneuvering among the bulrushes, they almost simultaneously noticed what appeared to be a very large, dark tree trunk moving under its own power through the lake weed. As they drew closer, however, they saw instead the twisting torso of some living animal. Its body, or, at any rate, what they could see of it above the surface, was massive and fleshy, fully as long as Ed's boat, at least. Both men said its pigmentation was spotted dark brown, resembling a pickerel.

The monster unexpectedly craned a long, muscular neck, topped by its large, horse-like head with serpentine features, its snake's eye regarding the awestruck fishermen. They snapped out of their terrified stupor only when the creature arched back its ungainly head in an obvious threat display and opened its gaping, red mouth. McKenzie and Seybert fell over themselves in comic, panicky efforts to row out of harm's way. Their hysterical splashing and cries for help were noticed by a friend on shore. He, too, saw the monster, grabbed a shotgun and leapt into his fastest sailboat. Perhaps feeling itself outnumbered, the saurian resident of the bulrushes abruptly plunged head-first into the water with a dramatic splash. By the time armed resistance reached the shaken fishermen, the creature had disappeared, "leaving the air all around heavy with a most sickening odor," according to one of the eyewitnesses.[1]

The 1887 encounter was neither the first nor the last time a sighting was made by area residents. As Lake Mills historian Mary Wilson has written, "Many people reported that they saw the monster raise its head from the waters. Its presence was a source of great worry and fear to the early residents. The sea monster who appeared every few years was recorded in our history by early citizens of great integrity and position in the community."[2] In time, with the apparent disappearance of the creature, worry and fear gave way to nostalgia for the old beast, who is still remembered by locals as "Rocky."

"Rocky"

Drawing by Jack Adair

His earliest documented sighting occurred in 1875. Ten years after the McKenzie-Seybert incident, a Mr. Hassam at first mistook the monster's corpulent torso for an outsized tree limb as he paddled among the same swampy lake weeds into which the hapless fishermen had unknowingly ventured. Raising its ponderous head only high enough above the water to get a brief look at the human intruder, it quickly sank beneath the surface. A similar sighting was reported before the turn of the century by a Mr. Harbeck, who lived on a hill overlooking the lake. A particularly dramatic confrontation took place about the same time with another Lake Mills resident, Fred Seaver. He was the only eyewitness to have seen the monster more than once. By far the more frightening of the two occasions occurred when "the animal seized his trolling hook and pulled his boat over half a mile at a rushing speed before he (the creature) let go." Perhaps Rocky was only being playful. In any case, Seaver's free ride represented the monster's final public appearance. Lake Mills underwent a population influx with attendant new construction during the 1920s. Maybe the lonely denizen of the waters moved on in search of lost solitude.

What is known about the immediate area suggests to some the monster's identity as a fugitive from the dinosaur age. Geological evidence shows the broad Midwestern plains were covered by a great, shallow, tropical sea during the warm periods between successive ice ages that moved back and forth across Wisconsin for millions of years. Was the creature in Rock Lake both a product and survivor of the state's deeply prehistoric epochs?

Curiously, the creature bears a strong resemblance to other, more famous counterparts in Scotland, upstate New York and Canada, implying not only its credibility, but the widespread nature of the lake-monster phenomenon. Moreover, Rocky's description, made nearly a hundred years before the Loch Ness Monster was known outside Europe, compares uncannily well with Nessie and her cousins elsewhere throughout the world. The existence of a large, unknown animal in Rock Lake has been underscored by reports of similar creatures scattered throughout the state. Brandon refers to "the many Wisconsin lakes with stories of monsters."[3]

For example, in Sturgeon Bay, on Lake Michigan, about 120 miles north of Rock Lake, residents still preserve the story of a great, hairy serpent that long ago carried away two sisters from the beach where they were bathing. Unusual, crocodile-like creatures have been actually recovered from untypical settings in Wisconsin. In 1892, a five-foot-plus specimen was found in the bank of the Rock River in Janesville, a few miles from Rock Lake. As recently as 1971, a thirty-inch crocodile was caught in a lake about sixty miles to the west.

Madison's Lake Mendota, forty miles west of Lake Mills, supposedly featured a dragonish creature that was seen in 1917 by a fisherman, who described its head as "snake-like." Later that same year, two students from the University at Madison claimed to have had a very close encounter with the beast, when its tongue flicked at the soles of their feet. Alleged sightings continued through the 1920s. Earlier seen in 1897, the monster was estimated to be twenty feet long.

There may, indeed, be some basis in fact for Rocky's existence, if not as a renegade dinosaur, then in the very real monsters known to glide through Wisconsin waters. During the summer of 1990, my fellow diver Jason Bucholtz was appalled to see a five-foot carp trailing behind us in Rock Lake. In the 1970s, engineers dynamiting an old pier at Lake Mendota, home of the dragon just described, accidentally killed a sturgeon that was a record-breaking twenty-five feet in length. Either one of these outsized specimens might qualify as the Monster of Rock Lake, while a similarly gargantuan fish or fishes could still be lurking in Tyranena's midnight depths.

There appear to be only four possible explanations for Rocky. It was a hoax, a genuine survivor from the age of dinosaurs, an abnormally large fish or some psychological phenomenon. A hoax seems unlikely, because many people saw the monster over at least a fifty-year period and none of the eyewitnesses ever sought to gain anything from their accounts. A dinosaur on the loose within the confines of Rock Lake is not so credible as some bloated old carp or a giant sturgeon mistaken for a plesiosaur from the Mesozoic Era. Even so, Rocky's resemblance to creatures from that period is unsettling.

A psychological interpretation seems more credible, however. Jungian psychologists, for example, believe recurrences such as the Rocky phenomenon are instances of an elemental human archetype, or subconscious vision common to the mind of man throughout the world, and they point to Loch Ness prototypes supposedly seen from Scotland to the Belgian Congo, from Siberia to Idaho as proof. Genetic memories from our earliest human or possibly even prehuman development, they argue, are triggered when we find ourselves in settings similar to and reminiscent of the environment in which we once, perhaps millions of years ago, were forced into indelibly traumatic confrontations of life and death with monstrous creatures. Or such visions may represent still deeper fears generated by our sense of physical inferiority in the animal world and our guilt for having technologically triumphed over that world. In other words, the lake monsters do not exist in the material realm, where their actual remains are never found and their unequivocal photographs never taken, but live instead in subconscious projections of our inner dread.

Such psychological interpretations are curiously paralleled by Native American explanations of the lake monster. Ho Chunk Indians who resided in the Lake Mills' area before the white settlers arrived told the newcomers that Rock Lake was inhabited by a "spirit guardian" placed there to protect the "rock tepees," the sacred graves of the "foreign shamans." With this local Native American tradition, the pyramids and the monster meet. Indeed, one seems to have been an extension of the other. Presumably, the creature's protective nature was known to the early European immigrants, whose receptive imaginations may have seen in a floating log or a gust of wind among the bulrushes the monstrous form of the spirit guardian.

Students of metaphysics believe an object or even a whole locality can be so supercharged by human emotion that a distinct feeling or atmosphere will linger around the thing or site long after the empowerment act, ceremony or ritual that infused it. Certain places radiate discernible emotional qualities, because of the peculiar nature of the deeds associated with them. When a whole community of people believe such things are possible and concentrate their conscious thoughts en masse to, say, the creation of a spirit guardian for their honored dead, the area may become suffused with a dynamic human impact felt by others even centuries later.

Remarkably, stamping an inanimate object or a specific place with a particular psychological image and/or feeling is no longer confined to paranormal speculations. Dr. Donald Roberts, a chemical engineer at the prestigious Getty Institute in Malibou, California, is at the forefront of the latest research into energy anomalies, and has demonstrated the very real interrelationship between altered states of human consciousness and the natural matrix structure of certain minerals.[4]

Complimenting his laboratory testing is the field research of Paul Devereux, organizer of the "Dragon Project," wherein instruments sensitive to ultra-low-frequency sounds and radiation levels were able to detect image-generating capabilities in the standing stones of various megalithic structures throughout Britain.[5]

Although not universally accepted by mainstream scientists, Roberts, Deveraux and others are accumulating persuasive evidence to show that sound, images and even human emotion may be encoded or recorded in natural materials which can be "played back," as it were, if triggered by the correct human input. Such encoding may have taken place at Rock Lake in the deeply prehistoric past, when shamans, who knew the secrets for storing images within the environment, implanted a "spirit guardian" to protect their people's City of the Dead.

In 1989, during our first side-scan sonar search of the lake bottom, a young Oneida Indian, unknown to any of us, asked permission to come aboard the *Sea Search*. During the voyage, he spoke infrequently and did not participate directly in our work. He did say, however, that he felt the presence of a protective spirit under the water and that it was a denizen of Rock Lake from ancient times, conjured there to keep the holy places from desecration. In fact, among the Ottawa, Chippewas, Saulteurs, Missisauges and apparently every other tribe throughout the Upper Peninsula, belief is still preserved in Bichi-Bichi, a supreme spirit guardian who dwells at the bottom of sacred lakes. Bichi-Bichi was no legendary convention, but seriously regarded as a dangerous being that received living sacrifice, usually in the form of dogs bound at jaws and legs, then thrown into the lake as offerings to the underwater beast.[6]

On this same mythic level, the Menomonie told of Michibissy, a deadly lake monster installed by the ancient miners to guard the waters around Isle Royale in the Upper Great Lakes for the protection of its rich copper deposits.

The creature is so strongly identified with these prehistoric civilizers that Michibissy represents the surviving spiritual energies of the dead "marine men," who sank back into the sea whence they came.[7] Coincidentally, a great serpent-guardian protected the cone-shaped stone pyramid in the Greek myth of Cadmus, which sheds unexpected light on the whole Rock Lake mystery. Both the ancient miners and Cadmus will be examined later.

The antiquity of Rock Lake's monster was suggested by a gargantuan effigy mound that skirted the south shore until its destruction in the 1920s. Dating back at least to the time that Aztalan flourished nine hundred years ago and described by *The Wisconsin Archaeologist* magazine as "a water-spirit," the eighty-four-foot-long earthwork portrayed some monstrous being dwelling in the lake. The mound did indeed indicate that such a creature was known at least on some level of experience to the early inhabitants of Rock Lake centuries before the arrival of modern European settlers.[8]

Certainly, many divers experience a "living presence" in the lake, a feeling of being watched. Worse, one sometimes feels like an intruder, a trespasser and not at all welcome. The Old Welsh word *hiraeth* describes an uncomfortable sensation of being in the wrong place at the worst time, when one's presence is far from desired. Hiraeth generally applies to the emotion divers encounter in Rock Lake, an emotion that may intensify to terror in its deepest, blackest parts, where all daylight is swallowed up in an impenetrable darkness, inkier than midnight. Confronted with such a lightless abyss, and in sharp, surreal contrast with the bright, green waters nearer the surface, it is all too easy to sense the massive, invisible guardian spirit lurking, waiting and watching from the frigid gloom. Several offerings to Rocky and propitiatory rituals on his behalf have been made over the years, but none have entirely succeeded in dispelling his protective aura over the sacred lake he prowls. A creature from the subconscious id, enduring hoax, elusive dinosaur, oversized carp or conjured spirit guardian, the Monster of Rock Lake lives on.

·12·

The Great Copper Mystery

*The People of the Sea have not only mingled their blood and
their strength with us all, but also are the traders who worked
the mines of Michigan during the age of bronze.*

—*L. Taylor Hansen*

S omeone took an awful lot of raw copper from North America a very
long time ago. Who was responsible for this and what they did with
it represent an enigma of vast proportions that investigators have
been puzzling over for more than a century, although most Americans are
unaware of the story.

Beginning around 3000 B.C., in excess of five hundred thousand tons of
copper were mined in Michigan's Upper Peninsula, with most activity taking place at Isle Royale, an island in Lake Superior on the Canadian border.
The mines abruptly and inexplicably shut down in 1200 B.C., reopening no
less mysteriously 2,300 years later. Until A.D. 1320, some additional two thousand tons were removed, destination unknown. As before, operations were
suddenly suspended for no apparent cause. Tools—mauls, picks, hammers,

shovels and levers—were left by their owners in place. Octave DuTemple, a foremost authority on early Michigan, asks, "Why did these miners leave their operations and implements as though planning on taking up their labors the next day, and yet mysteriously never returned?"[1]

William P. F. Ferguson writes, "The work is of a colossal nature," and "amounted to the turning over of the whole formation to their depth and moving many cubic acres—it would not be seriously extravagant to say cubic miles—of rock."[2]

The prehistoric mines were no crude holes in the ground, but incredibly efficacious operations to extract staggering masses of raw material as quickly as possible. An average of 1,000 to 1,200 tons of ore were excavated per pit, yielding about one hundred thousand pounds of copper each.[3] To achieve such prodigious yields, the miners employed simple techniques that enabled them to work with speed and efficiency. They created intense fires atop a copper-bearing vein, heated the rock to very high temperatures, then doused it with water. The rock fractured and stone tools were employed to extract the copper. Deep in the pits, a vinegar mixture was used to speed spalling and reduce smoke.

The ancient enterprise was a mind-boggling affair, including about five thousand mines mostly along the Keweenaw Peninsula and the eastern end of Lake Superior above the St. Mary's River. On the northern shore, the diggings extended 150 miles, varying in width from four to seven miles, through the Trap Range, to include three Michigan counties (Keweenaw, Houghton and Ontonagon). At Isle Royale, the mining area was forty miles long and averaged five miles across. The pits ran in practically a contiguous line for thirty miles through the Rockland region, as they did at greater intervals in the Ontonagon District. If all these pits were put end to end single file they would form a man-made trench more than five miles long, twenty feet wide and thirty feet deep.[4]

Estimates of ten thousand men working the mines for a thousand years seem credible, as does the conclusion that they were not slaves, because the miners carried away their dead.[5] No ancient graves nor evidence of cremations have been found in the Upper Peninsula. Indeed, virtually all they left behind were their tools, literally millions of them. As far back as the 1840s, ten wagonloads of stone hammers were taken from a single location near Rockland. Those in McCargo Cove, on the north side of Isle Royale, amounted to one thousand tons.[6] The mauls were mass-produced in various sizes and types to serve different tasks. Some were only two-and-a-quarter-pound hand-held tools for finishing and shaping. Others weighed forty pounds and more. Fastened to cables suspended from a cross-bar, they were swung like pendulums to batter the rock face and crush chunks of ore. Most hammers were five to ten pounds, grooved to fit a wooden handle tied around the middle. Generally egg-shaped, they were made of diabase, a hard, tough, fine-grained igneous rock.

W. H. Holmes succinctly writes, "It is unlikely, however, that any considerable amount of the shaping work was conducted on the island (Isle Royale). It seems to me more likely that the pieces of metal obtained were carried away to distant centers of population to be worked by skilled artisans and we may justly assume that a considerable trade existed in the raw material."[7] Those "distant centers of population" were Rock Lake and Aztalan, which were connected to the Great Lakes mining areas by a belt of similar mounds. One Upper Peninsula temple-mound was ten feet tall, fifteen feet long at the sides and virtually identical to Aztalan's Pyramid of the Moon. As we shall see, the ancient copper miners and the inhabitants of Rock Lake-Aztalan were one and the same people.

America's ancient copper mines represent the key to unlocking Rock Lake's deepest secrets. The grandiose mining enterprise began suddenly around 3000 B.C. and terminated just as abruptly 1,800 years later. Investigators believe that the mines were functioning at their peak capacity during the last three centuries of operations, the same period when Rock Lake's pyramids adorned its early shoreline.

Rock Lake was an ancient mining center, a clearing-house where raw copper extracted from the Great Lakes Region was readied for shipment elsewhere and home for the miners until they could return to Michigan the following summer. To precisely regulate all the stages of procedure in those widespread operations, involving thousands of miners, handlers, sailors and workers of all kinds, an efficient, calendrical technology was vital to success and survival; hence, the abundant astronomically significant structures stretching from Rock Lake to the Upper Peninsula.

When prehistoric America's copper mining ceased all at once in 1200 B.C., the Michigan pits were abandoned for the next twenty-one centuries. They were suddenly reopened in A.D. 900, an event that can only mean that, despite the virtual abandonment of the Rock Lake area for thousands of years, it was continuously held in profound awe by numerous successive generations. In their mythology the lake had achieved a powerfully sacred status that continues to this day among tribes as widespread as the Menomonie and the Yaqui.

The date for reopening Michigan's mines is enormously significant, because it coincides with the establishment of Cahokia, the greatest city in ancient North America. The overlords of Cahokia were as interested in copper as their fourteenth-century-B.C. ancestors in Wisconsin. Their pyramidal burials in the prehistoric megalopolis of south central Illinois are rich in copper armor and ornaments.

But personal wealth accounted for only a small fraction of the tons of imported mineral. Alliance with another mound-building people at Spiro, Oklahoma, near the Arkansas River, provided portage to Mesoamerica trade centers. The Spiro seamen operated three-masted, thirty-foot-long wooden vessels plying the Gulf of Mexico to Florida and Vera Cruz.

Cahokia, like older Rock Lake, had its astronomers, whose Woodhenge, a precisely arranged circle of red-painted cedar posts, enabled calculation of the positions of the sun. Thus provided with celestial information, they knew when to dispatch their mining expeditions to the Upper Peninsula. Doubtless the site chosen for the construction of Cahokia had been originally determined by its central location at the hub of trade routes converging from all over the continent.

When Cahokia's society collapsed in A.D. 1100, much of its culture-bearing population migrated naturally to the Rock Lake area in order to get as close as possible to the copper-bearing regions, because the mineral had become their chief trade good with the Toltec civilizations of Mexico. Commercial routes traveled by Spiro sailors may even have extended as far as South America. The Andean civilizations of the Chimu and other pre-Inca peoples used copper on a large scale, although proportionate natural supplies did not occur in Peru.

Referring to the implements first encountered by Columbus during his fourth trip to the New World, Roy Ward Drier writes, "That the copper from which these tools, scattered over such a vast area of country, were manufactured, came from the ancient mines of Lake Superior, does not admit of doubt. Although large and numerous deposits of copper ore are scattered through Arizona, New Mexico, Mexico and Central and South America, there is no evidence that the aborigines had sufficient metallurgical knowledge or skill to reduce the ores to refined copper. The shores of Lake Superior have the only known workable deposits of native copper in the world. The term virgin copper is well used to denote its purity. In this latter day, it outranks all others in the markets of the world."[8]

Archaeological excavations in the 1930s at Aztalan discovered the remains of a large rectangular building containing an abundance of unworked copper, establishing the site's identity as a mining town. A long, broad roll of matting for storage had been thoroughly stained with green impregnations from the minerals. The building's eight-inch-thick walls were curved slightly and ran between two large furnaces or fire pits, all suggesting that the copper was cast into ingots before shipment.[9] As long ago as 1936, so-called "Indian shafts" were observed on the floor of Rock Lake. Again in the 1990s, divers found several unusually large depressions at the bottom, usually if not always near a stone monument. Although they resemble pits dug by the ancient miners of Isle Royale, their depth is indeterminable, because they are largely filled in with silt. No one has been able to define what natural process might be responsible for these depressions, which have all the earmarks of man-made features and compare almost exactly in circumference to the Aztalan furnaces or fire pits.

The ancient mines explain why a civilization at Rock Lake came about. Tyranena was at the pivot point and the crossroads in the prehistoric copper trade. The raw minerals were extracted from the Michigan pits during the short summer season and transported to Rock Lake for collection and casting in preparation for shipment. That the ancient inhabitants of Rock Lake were in fact the same people who mined copper in the Upper Peninsula there can be little doubt. While no burials exist throughout their vast mining district, around the shores of Rock Lake were in excess of seventy grave-mounds containing the remains of unknown thousands of ancient dead, some interred, many others cremated, and identifiably associated with the prehistoric miners. Among the best preserved examples were the bones of a man accompanied by a pebble-hammer of the exact kind found throughout Isle Royale, where such tools were used in finishing the extracted copper, flattening spurs and trimming off sharp edges. The miner had been buried in a conical earth-mound on the south shore of Rock Lake, doubtless like his fellow workers still lying under its waters beneath identical structures of stone.[10] Workers who died on the job in the copper mines of Michigan were brought back to be buried in Tyranena's necropolis. Investigators have sought Isle Royale's ancient cemetery for more than one hundred years. They need only look as far as Rock Lake.

·13·

Revelation in the Canary Islands

In Fourteen Hundred and Ninety Two,
Columbus sailed the ocean blue,
To prove that the old maps were true.
—*Child's nursery rhyme of unknown provenance*

In the summer of 1990, I sailed among the Canary Islands, off the coast of Morocco, still in pursuit of answers to "the Atlantis Problem." The Canaries have nothing at all to do with charming, little, yellow birds, but derive partly from the Latin *canari,* "dogs." When Roman ships visited the islands in the second century B.C., the original inhabitants revered the dog as a sacred being. But the Canary Islanders already referred to themselves as "Canari" long before the Romans arrived.[1] The name appears to have had a similar meaning in both Latin and the native speech, which was a mixed Indo-European language with at least several Latin cognates.[2]

Previous to the first century A.D., the Atlantic group was known throughout the Mediterranean World as the Blessed Isles, the Fortunate Isles, the
Hesperides or the Isles of the Blessed. Forgotten after the fall of classical civilization, they were isolated from outside contact for almost a thousand years
until their rediscovery by Portuguese sailors in the fourteenth century. The
Canari more commonly referred to themselves as *Guanches* (simply, "men"),
a once civilized race that had slowly degenerated over millennia of inter-
breeding, while their level of society slid back, quite literally, into the caves
and they reverted to troglodytes. These Paleolithic primitives could not stand
up to the firearms of the conquistadors, and the islands have since been the
colonial possession of Spain.

Before their virtual extermination, some studies were made of the
Guanches, a white people, often fair-complected and light eyed, not infrequently of tall stature, with red, auburn and occasionally blond hair. Despite
their genetically debased condition, they preserved traditions from long-
gone ages of civilized greatness and still gathered at the ruined stone monuments of their ancestors for special events. Some of these cyclopean walls,
called *tagora*, survive as crumbling rectangular enclosures, circles and even
pyramids.

At Santa Cruz, capital of Tenerife, largest of the islands, I was surprised to
learn that regular, ancient contacts between the Canaries and North America
were generally acknowledged by the academic community. Talk of possible
pre-Columbian visitors from Europe is tabu throughout professional circles
in the United States, but Tenerife's leading historical scholar, Professor Lopez
Herrera, writes, "One fact about which we may be certain is that there existed
a relation in ancient times between the people of Canarian origin and the
inhabitants of America."[3]

He goes on to cite abundant evidence for Guanche presence in North
America dating to the early European Bronze Age. Outstanding among that
evidence is the inscription on a strange artifact found in Ohio, the famous

Grove Creek Stone. Its characters correspond almost exactly to written carvings in the Canary Island of Hierro. Underscoring this undeniable correspondence were the terra-cotta grains recovered from the Grove Creek barrow; their resemblance to similar grains in numerous burial caves throughout the Canaries was unmistakable. Of all the arguments made in favor of overseas contacts between the European ancient world and America, the Grove Creek Stone is the most persuasive physical evidence.[4]

A comparison of petroglyphic signs in prehistoric North America and the Canary Islands additionally supports a relationship between them. Many of the individual signs, such as an inverted barbell-like figure (expressing the highest and lowest position of the sun), occur on both sides of the Atlantic and signify the same meanings.[5]

And I wondered about the mysterious barbell object found by Doug Gossage at Rock Lake's Limnatis pyramid. Most pertinent to our Rock Lake investigation was the even closer parallel between incised symbols found at Lake Superior's Isle Royale, site of pre-Columbian copper mining, and the same signs scattered throughout Hierro and La Palma. Comparison of skulls belonging to the ancient Americans with Guanche examples strongly reinforced the idea of physical contact with the European world. In Dr. Herrera's words, "There was a perfect correspondence between the characteristics shown by the Canary craniums and those of the two brought by Mr. Simonin." (George Simonin was a field researcher for the Paris Geographic Society who retrieved a pair of Native American skulls in 1874.)[6]

Proof of North American-Canary Island contacts is abundant and exceeds the parameters of this book. But I was sufficiently impressed with the evidence, especially the incontrovertible links with Michigan's ancient mining territories, to pursue my research in the Canaries with an eye toward their bearing on Rock Lake, if any.

From Tenerife, I took a ferry to Lanzarote, which is 125 miles closer to North Africa than any of the rest of the seven islands. After docking at the capital port of Arrecefe and checking into my hotel, I walked through the ocean-front park, intent only on some casual sightseeing, when I was thunderstruck to confront the very object that had been sought in the depths of Rock Lake for more than fifty years: a twenty-foot-tall conical pyramid. Incredibly, it exactly matched Max Nohl's description of the sunken structure he had encountered in 1937 under the south end of the lake.

I could hardly believe what I was seeing. Before me rose a pyramid of rough stones chosen for size and only mortared in a few places, six feet across at the base, in the shape of an inverted ice-cream cone. The sole difference lay in the stones themselves: the Lanzarote pyramid is made of volcanic rock, with which the island abounds; river stones make up Max Nohl's Cone. Otherwise, the American and Canary Island features were perfectly identical. In all my travels throughout Europe and studies of classical and preclassical societies, I had never found so much as a reference to a conical stone pyramid such as this one, and, as far as I knew, nothing of the kind existed anywhere else except under the waters of Rock Lake.

During my stay in Lanzarote, I learned that the large stone cone was only one of unknown numbers which had originally dotted the island until after the Norman conquest of the fifteenth century. The prehistoric capital of the island, known to the Guanches as Zonzamas, is presently an archaeological area high on a very windy hill surrounded by volcanoes and overlooking a desolate plain to the sea. But enough of its ruins still exist to show that Zonzamas was once, at the time of the Trojan War (1240 to 1230 B.C.), a magnificent headquarters for the Mency, or ruler of Lanzarote.

The cyclopean construction of a cave-like citadel; several broad, squarish, partially subterranean structures; and the layout of interconnecting rooms forming the palace all bespoke a centralized authority precisely the same as other Bronze Age power centers I had visited only weeks before in Crete, Troy and Greek Mycenaea. What distinguished Zonzamas from the others, however, was a large, cone-shaped pyramid, originally about twenty

*The cone pyramid in the capital of Arrecefe, near
the western shore of Lanzarote, in the Canary Islands.*

feet tall. Unlike its Arrecefe counterpart, however, the Zonzamas pyramid had fallen over on one side, doubtless a result of the many earthquakes that shake this seismically active island. Approaching it laterally, I was struck by its resemblance to some of the more amorphous stone features I had encountered on the bottom of Rock Lake, and I wondered if they, like this prostrate colossus, had fallen since their abandonment.

Some distance away, but still within the archaeological zone, I found at least a dozen circular piles of stone, the remains of smaller, cone-shaped pyramids. I was at once reminded of the circular stone heap I had found two years before in the southeast quadrant of Rock Lake. During that dive, I had removed the squared stone, a man-made brick, that we believed might have come from the base of a conical structure. Looking at the nearly identical remnants of the cone-shaped pyramids of Zonzamas, I could no longer doubt our original idea.

Returning to the Arrecefe cone at noon, only a few days after the summer solstice, I saw that it cast virtually no shadow. I wondered if these conical structures were not, in addition to their function as burial monuments, sundials to mark precise information about the position of the sun with sharply defined shadows thrown by their pointed apexes. Dr. Scherz had already suggested the celestial alignments of Rock Lake's submerged features, and the Arrecefe pyramid seemed to confirm his ideas.

The cone-pyramid design, so unusual in itself, did indeed recur throughout Lanzarote as nowhere else, and I thought back to the very few other references in the ancient world to such a unique structure. Although no conical pyramids have so far been found in Egypt, representations of them survive in Egyptian funeral art. They were invariably associated with the Far West of Anubis, as though the spirit-guardian were striding from that direction. The Egyptian cone's only known function was as a symbol for the realm of the deceased, the spiritual otherworld. It is otherwise entirely mysterious.

Egyptian temple art typically depicting the deceased taken in charge by the dog-headed Anubis, spirit guide to the afterlife. Behind him and the inscription from the Book of the Dead *stands the mysterious, copper-colored cone pyramid.*

Even so, its juxtaposition to the dog-headed god of the dead parallels the canine funerary rites conducted among the cone-shaped monuments of both the Canary Islands and Rock Lake, both in the Far West, symbolized by the Egyptian cone. That the Egyptians were aware of these mortuary rituals and symbols enough to include them in their own funeral ceremonies implies that they were familiar with the ocean-going metallurgists and merchants who provided the copper for their tools and weapons in the Nile's Chalcolithic or Copper Age.

It may be significant, therefore, that whenever the cone pyramid appears in Egyptian temple art it is always copper colored. In fact, the Egyptians referred to the predynastic invasion of the Nile Delta by a seafaring people from the distant West they knew as the Mesentiu, or "metal workers," from their word for "foundry," *mesnet.* It was this metal-working Mesentiu who established Egypt's first royal family, an event reproduced often in Egyptian art as the falcon-headed sun-god, Horus, wielding a harpoon from his boat against a hippopotamus, symbol of the predynastic natives.[7]

A truly startling and convincing connection between ancient Egypt, Lanzarote and Rock Lake exists in the humble figure of man's best friend. Roman visitors in the second century B.C. referred to the Canary Islanders as the *Canarii*, or "Dog People," as mentioned earlier, because the natives venerated the dog as a cult animal in a mystery religion resembling the Egyptians belief in Anubis, the dog-headed spirit guide who led souls from the material world through death into the afterlife.

The Guanches worshiped their dog god near the base of a stone conical pyramid and interred dogs in sacred cemeteries accompanied by elaborate funeral rites. The only other parallel to such canine reverence occurred in Pharaonic Egypt, at Cynopolis, or "Dog City," where literally tens of thousands of mummified dogs were buried over the course of centuries.

Remarkably, this same unusual cult flourished in Aztalan, where dogs were the only animals domesticated by the inhabitants.[8] They provided the creatures with ritual funerals, including grave goods in the form of intentionally broken pottery symbolizing mourning and the end of physical existence. The dog was identically revered at Angel Mounds, Aztalan's sister city, on the banks of the Ohio River in southern Indiana.[9]

Aztalan and Angel Mounds were inhabited by people belonging to the same culture, immigrants who came from the Mississippian megalopolis at Cahokia after the turn of the twelfth century. Their affectionate, even reverential, attitude toward the animal sharply separated them from the resident Plains Indians. The Ottawa, for example, offered living dogs as sacrifices, often binding the legs and jaws and then throwing the hapless creatures into a lake to appease Bichi-Bichi, the monster they believed dwelt under water.[10]

Clearly, the civilizers of Aztalan were not the same people who hunted and gathered outside the walled enclosure. Even so, the Aztalaners' vener-

Lake Tirajana in Gran Canaria, Canary Islands.
Note ruined stone wall in the foreground.

ation of the dog as the center of a mystery cult formed an intriguing parallel with similar if not identical worship in Egypt and the Atlantic Isles of
the Blessed.

But ancient America's connection with the Canary Islands did not end
with my stay on Lanzarote. From the port of Arrecefe, I sailed to Gran
Canaria, as different from Lanzarote as the Alps are from the Sahara. Whereas
rectangular Lanzarote is low and bleak, with great, black lava fields, circular Gran Canaria is precipitously high with mountains and deep with lush
valleys. At the excellent La Palma museum, I studied a map of the island.

The name of a place near the center of Gran Canaria caught my eye:
Tirajana. I thought of Rock Lake's Tiranena and resolved to drive there the
next day.

For the rest of the afternoon, I strolled aimlessly through the old part of
the capital and came across the Casa de Colon, actually the governor's man-

sion, in which Christopher Columbus stayed just before sailing for the New World on his maiden transatlantic voyage. The house was perfectly preserved, and I was fascinated by the masterly crafted models of the admiral's famous little sailing vessels.

But I was to learn about more than early Spanish ship design. A professional source at the Casa de Colon told me a very curious tale that would have a completely unexpected bearing on my forthcoming visit to the island's Tirajana. The story, according to my well-read informant, was something of a badly kept secret, but all the documentation was available for anyone with patience enough to page through reams of late-fifteenth- and early-sixteenth-century documents, all handwritten in stylized, archaic Castillian and church Latin, at the Barcelona archives. In any case, the account concerns Christopher Columbus and his stay at the governor's mansion in Gran Canaria.

Being a true Renaissance scholar, the Genoese navigator studied all available information about the possibility of a transoceanic expedition. Some of that information included the traditions of earlier seafaring peoples, such as the Vikings, who sailed into the distant West. Most historians believe he knew of the sea routes taken by Leif Ericson, Thorfinn Karlsefni and other Scandinavian seamen, but he rejected a northern crossing when he found a colonial report made shortly after the Spanish subjugation of Gran Canaria, around 1470.

In the military report, a Guanche chief named Tirajana claimed that his ancestors were far greater sailors than the Spaniards, because they traveled regularly to the end of the ocean, over the horizon of the sunset to a great land. Although the Spanish officer who wrote the report dismissed the Guanche chief's statement as the defiant boast of a defeated man, Columbus felt the old native's claim merited further investigation, and he set sail for Gran Canaria. At the governor's house, arrangements were made for a trip to the mountainous interior of the island with an interpreter. In a few days, he reached the former native kingdom of Tirajana, where he met with one of the last surviving members of the Guanche royal family. Through a Spanish translator, he repeated to Columbus the same tradition of transatlantic voyages made by his ancestors and told him additionally of a great underwater stream that carried their ships directly from their island home across the sea to the great land in the West. The Guanche survivor also provided stellar navigation, as preserved in the oral tradition of a tribal song about his ancestors, with particular reference to the Pleiades, to the far country beyond the evening twilight.

Convinced he had heard the truth, Columbus sailed away with the old Guanche's information. The rest is history. Or almost. The Tirajana contribution to his discovery was subsequently suppressed by either the Church authorities or by Columbus himself, because he did not want to share the glory of 1492 with anyone else.

The jealousy with which he protected his achievements is well known, but the motivation of the Church is far more credible. To admit that a heathen and the member of an inferior race just conquered by Catholic Spain had provided invaluable sailing directions to a Christian admiral would have been ideologically unacceptable in the extreme. Enterline asks quite correctly, "What Renaissance Spanish scholar having any political sense would give a second thought to publishing anything detrimental to his sovereign's claims?"[11]

So all that was left to official history was Columbus's visit to the governor's mansion previous to his departure from Gran Canaria for the New World. The conspiracy of silence, so the argument goes, has been maintained by the Spanish authorities to the present day, because of the disruptive independence movement still active in the Canary Islands, whose radical leaders could use the story of Tirajana as political propaganda for their separatist cause. Such propaganda might also prove especially effective during the five hundredth anniversary of Spain's discovery of the New World, an event of powerful significance throughout Iberia, Latin America and, indeed, the whole civilized world.

In any case, the story does not lack for some disquieting details that tend to confirm a Canary Island role in the Columbus enigma that still intrigues investigators after half a millennium. For example, the "great underwater stream" the native said went straight to the other side of the ocean does indeed exist. It is the Canary Island Current that runs from Gran Canaria to the shores of Central America and the Bahamas, where Columbus made his landfall. In fact, his ships rode the Canary Island Current across the Atlantic, just as the old Guanche said his ancestors used to do long ago.

The man who supposedly translated for Columbus was called de Aranya. Interestingly, a Diego de Aranya did sail on the *Santa Maria* to "New Spain," where he was employed with success as an interpreter and eventually promoted to Alguazil of the Fleet. Today, the colonial town of De Aranya lies within the former Guanche kingdom of Tirajana.

Born in Cordoba, Diego de Aranya settled on land purchased in Gran Canaria, where he mastered the native language and translated the deposed native chief's transatlantic sailing instructions for Columbus. Diego died in a massacre of about forty other Spaniards on the island of Espanola.[12] He was survived by his cousin, Pedro, who captained a ship on the third voyage from Spain to the New World and retired to Gran Canaria's Tirajana.

Columbus may even have heard about the old Guanche voyages from his own wife, Beatrix Enriquez, whose maiden name was de Aranya. In any case, the de Aranya who allegedly translated native accounts of transatlantic crossings was undoubtedly the same man as Columbus's interpreter in the New World and whose cousin dwelt at the area in question, Tirajana.

The logbook of the admiral's first voyage to "New Spain" is replete with sometimes cryptic references to the Canary Islands. In his entry for Thursday, August 9, he wrote that the "natives of the island of Hierro declared that every year they saw land to the west of the Canaries. And others, natives of Gomera [centermost of the Canary Islands] affirmed the same on oath."[13]

Columbus knew perfectly well that no continent could be seen from the Canaries. More significantly, he admitted to having been in contact with the Guanches about a land across the sea. His entry of Saturday, October 13, the day after he landed in the Bahamas, discussed the Indian inhabitants of Espanola. He compared their skin to "the color of the Canarians. Nor should anything else be expected, as this island is in a line east and west from the island of Hierro in the Canaries."[14] Remarkably, he let slip here his total lack of surprise at finding that the natives of the New World and the Guanches apparently belonged to the same race, implying transatlantic contacts time out of mind before the Spanish arrival.

In fact, the Arawak Indians themselves told the Spanish explorers that they were not the first white people to visit their islands. Las Casas, a contemporary of Columbus, who interviewed many aboriginal inhabitants of Cuba, reported, "The neighboring Indians of that island asserted that there arrived to this island of Hispaniola other bearded men like ourselves, not long ago."[15] The Arawaks' conception of time was entirely vague, so events still part of their folk tradition might have seemed to them relatively recent.

Evidence for pre-Columbian visits from bearded white men is not confined to native accounts. Significantly, some of that evidence identifies a distinct Canary Island presence throughout Middle America. Among the most revealing and convincing comparisons appears on a Chac-mool, or statue of the Mayas' preeminent deity, Chac, their rain-god. His stone effigy found at Chichen Itza, Yucatan's foremost ceremonial center, portrayed the god wearing peculiarly designed sandals that are "exact representations of those found on the feet of the Guanches."[16]

The ancient Canary Islanders were known to ritually sacrifice a select group of virgins, the *harimagadas,* by drowning them in a cenote, or natural well, to appease the water gods. The Mayans practiced the same rite at Chichen Itza, where the "Cenote of Sacrifice" and the Guanche footwear are found.

Interestingly, *tinya* is a North African disease that still appears among some Berbers and a few modern inhabitants of the Canary Islands, usually mixed descendants of the Guanches, who were known to suffer from the malady. Physicians accompanying the conquistadors treated the natives of Yucatan for tinya, which had already taken root in the New World before the arrival of the Spaniards.

The *Lagenaria siceraria* is a bottle gourd that was similarly cultivated by the Guanaches and the pre-Columbian peoples of Mesoamerica. Valid cultural and material comparisons between the ancient inhabitants of the Canary Islands and the natives of Middle America are as numerous as they are convincing.

A highly civilized people who controlled Ecuador before the Incas called themselves the "Canari." They were South America's most accomplished seafarers, who sailed ocean-going balsa vessels, each able to transport freight in excess of thirty tons, northward along the western coasts of Mexico to Mazatlan and south as far as Chile.[17] The Canari introduced the concept of "axe-money," axe-shaped copper currency, throughout Mesoamerican and Andean societies, where axe-monies became the basis of pre-Columbian monetary systems. Their capital, Chincha, on the south-central coast of Peru, was inhabited by six thousand merchantmen. The name of this port city is especially intriguing in light of our investigation: it appears related to Chibcha Chia, the Canari moon-goddess who caused the Great Flood that drowned the island motherland of their ancestors.[18] Chibcha Chia was not an exclusively Canari deity, however, and was venerated throughout the Incan Empire even after the Spanish conquest.

The Ecuadoran Canari were also mound builders who constructed pyramidal earthworks *(tolas)* as part of a death cult, farmed thousands of acres of raised fields and worked in large quantities of copper, going so far as to actually manufacture bronze. These features are especially similar to prehistoric activities at Wisconsin's Aztalan, whose own connection with the Canary Islands will be examined in a forthcoming chapter. Indeed, the Ecuadoran

Canari's resemblance to the Canari (Guanches) of the Canary Islands, in name as well as culture, suggests a veritable transatlantic presence in America many centuries before Columbus.

David Tsukernik, one of Russia's leading philologists and historians, examined the papers of the most important contributors to Columbus's New World expedition, particularly those written by the officers of his crew. He points out that the chart Columbus used to find the Americas was filled with abundant facts about the mid-Atlantic not available to fifteenth-century Europeans and displayed navigational information which could only have been derived from previous transoceanic voyages.[19]

Donwith underscores Tsukernik's conclusions with evidence that the distance Columbus expected to cross was in fact the exact nautical mileage of his "Voyage of Discovery."[20] Even the supposed conspiracy of silence between the Spanish Crown and the Catholic Church to deny all credit to the old Guanche's vital assistance is not without support. An eminent historian of the Renaissance, Stefansson, argues that Alexander VI Borgia, the new and intensely politically active pope, connived with the Madrid governmental authorities to conceal all collected information about the opposite continent previous to the Columbus voyage in order to secure Catholic Spain's title to the new territories.[21] It was this right-of-title that was their chief motivation in heralding the discovery as a purely Catholic enterprise.

Enterline writes, "As soon as a nation discovers new lands, it has new political problems on its hands as well as new assets in the face of possible competition from other nations. When several nations make similar discoveries and the geographical situation of none of these discoveries is quite clear, the problem can become complex indeed."[22]

In view of the profuse evidence demonstrating Canary Island contacts with prehistoric America, a Guanche tradition of transatlantic voyages is at least plausible. The old nursery rhyme quoted at the head of this chapter seems to allude to as much. To what "old maps" did Columbus refer?

Even the origins of this nursery rhyme are obscure. Did it suggest, perhaps sarcastically, something that was at least suspected long ago; namely, that the admiral was privy to secret information from older sources?

"Those who choose to," argues Enterline, "are therefore still free to imagine Columbus setting out blindly on a voyage which, without the intervention of Providence and a new continent, would have led him, his associates and their loyal crews to certain death and their King and Queen to ridicule. The rest of us must bide our time until the next discovery in a random, unknown library of some dusty manuscript unread in recent centuries, or until some new insight into existing records appears."[23] Perhaps that "dusty manuscript" proving the Guanche contribution to Columbus's voyage of discovery may someday be found in the Barcelona archives.

My drive through the interior of Gran Canaria was a spectacular trip along a road winding ever higher up into thickly forested mountains and beautifully bizarre countryside molded by millennia of volcanic activity. Among the highest, most solitary peaks, I reached the weirdly configured Roche Nublo, the Umbilicus, or Navel Stone, a gargantuan, dagger-like prominence of rock thrust up toward heaven from the very center of the island. On its opposite, western side, the land sloped down into lush valleys, eventually leading to the sea.

The serpentine road curved into the little town of De Aranya, discussed above, and beyond to Tirajana. From the high road overlooking the former Guanche kingdom, I saw a small body of water reminiscent of Rock Lake. I scouted around its shoreline and found the ruined battlements of drystone, cyclopean structures, some of them maintained by modern farmers to prevent hillside erosion. But little imagination was needed to envision at least part of the ancient splendor that once graced this valley.

For three years, I had been intrigued by the Ho Chunk name for Rock Lake, Tyranena, particularly because I was unable to learn anything about it from any Native American sources. The word does not translate into any

Indian language. The departing Indians told white settlers of the 1830s that the little lake was called "Tyranena," although they had no idea what the name meant, only that it was an ancient appellation belonging to a former people in residence in the Lake Mills vicinity.

"Tyranena" does not even sound Indian. In three years of search for some parallel name among Native American peoples and throughout everything I could learn about the European Bronze Age, only in the name of a Guanche royal family did I find a valid comparison—a comparison that even extended to a physical resemblance between the two lakes.

Incredibly, the Canary Island lake of Tirajana is similar in size and even in outline to its Wisconsin counterpart—not as it appears today, but as it existed 3,500 years ago, according to the hydrological study described in Dr. Scherz's 1989 report.[24]

Given the otherwise unique, cone-shaped stone pyramids of Lanzarote; the abundant, valid material evidence supporting prehistoric North American contacts with La Palma and Hierro; the unmistakable parallel between the Canari of the Canary Islands and the Canari of Peru; Christopher Columbus's probable sailing instructions from a Guanche at Tirajana; that name's singular resemblance to Tyranena and even the physical similarity of both lakes, a major part of the Rock Lake mystery had been solved to my own personal satisfaction. Pondering all this alone at the tranquil shore of Tirajana, surrounded by the stone remnants of a forgotten civilization, I tried to envision a believable scenario for what took place thirty-five centuries ago.

An expedition of seafarers belonging to the royal family of Tirajana, in what is now the De Aranya region of Gran Canaria, sailed across the Atlantic, riding the Canary Island Current into the Caribbean and along the east coast of North America. They entered what is now the St. Lawrence Seaway, then much more navigable, and proceeded to the upper Great Lakes, the destination of their long voyage. Participating in Isle Royale's copper mining operations, the Bronze Age Canari were not discoverers. They used the star charts and other navigational aids long before developed by their forefathers, who made the first transatlantic runs to America from the beginning of the fourth millennium B.C.

The Tirajana seamen mined the Upper Peninsula during the summer months. With the onset of cold weather, they navigated the inland water-ways to a mining outpost just below the heavy snow line and centrally located to serve as a clearing-house for the copper trade. Near this outpost, they dis-covered a small lake with a superficial resemblance to Lake Tirajana, back in Gran Canaria. In commemoration, they gave it the same name and rein-forced its identity by burying their dead along its shoreline under the same kind of cone-shaped stone pyramids typical of their home culture.

Complementing their funerary purposes, the structures were oriented to various celestial phenomena—phases of the moon tracked by the tent-like mounds and solar solstices cast by the pointing shadows of the conical pyramids. The visibly recurring cycles of the heavens were linked with the cyclical patterns of birth-death-rebirth of the human soul, as explained by the Bronze Age mystery cults practiced throughout the preclassical Euro-pean world. Synchronous with their religious functions, the sky alignments provided invaluable information for trips to and from the copper-mining regions, coinciding with the end of spring and the advent of winter.

Astronomical data controlled by the leaders of this imported society told farmers when to plant and harvest their crops, seamen when to take advantage of various sailing seasons, shamans when they could conduct their rituals or kings when they might be crowned. Knowledge was power, and the "foreign chiefs," as they were to be remembered through genera-tions of Native American tradition, established in ancient Wisconsin a sacred center of immense influence at their lake site.

"Tirajana" changed only slightly in the mouths of the local Plains Indi-ans, whose language did not allow a duplicate pronunciation of the Indo-European word, and it became "Tyranena." The local tribespeople undoubtedly traded hides and meat with the foreigners, and may even have been employed as laborers in building the stone monuments, long since sent to the bottom of Rock Lake.

In a short time, Tirajana-Tyranena became a flourishing clearing-house for raw copper brought from the upper Great Lakes. The valuable mineral was stored and prepared for shipment before being sent down the Rock River to the Mississippi, out into the Gulf of Mexico and across the Atlantic Ocean to preclassical European metal-smiths, who fashioned the weapons and luxury goods of the Bronze Age. When that Age came to an abrupt halt around 1200 B.C., the mines of the Upper Peninsula were abandoned, the copper trade ceased altogether and the "foreign chiefs" went back to Gran Canaria.

But they could not leave the stone shrines, temples and tombs of their dead family members unprotected. Before they shipped out, they excavated a canal to a tributary of the Rock River running east and west just north of the sacred precinct. A deluge rushed into the little lake, dramatically raising its level and drowning all the monuments and graves, save perhaps for the tops of a few on higher ground, under forty to sixty feet of water. Satisfied that the natives would be unable to defile the bones of their kinsmen, the Canarians returned to their homeland, far across the sea.

So then did I return home, inwardly satisfied that the Tyranena of Rock Lake had been identified thirty-five centuries ago with the Tirajana of Gran Canaria.

·14·

The Serpent People

The serpent power was the one that worked the mines of Michigan for copper, Peru and England for tin, manufactured their product on their own island and sold it or traded it for food and other products.

—*L. Taylor Hansen*

Cadmus was the young prince of Phoenicia, the Land of Purple, the biblical Canaan, so named after the exquisite purple dye manufactured from a rare mollusk (the *Purpura murex*) found along the shores of what is now known as Lebanon. Cadmus had a sister, Europa, who one day saw a white bull emerging from the sea. As she approached the magnificent creature, it lay down in supplication at her feet. In a playful mood, she got onto its back and bade it rise. The bull instantly stood up and dashed into the water, carrying Europa toward the setting sun. Hearing her cries for help, Cadmus set sail to rescue his sister. But the powerful bull swam too fast and was eventually lost to sight.

The prince voyaged to Delphi, Apollo's supreme oracle in the Gulf of Corinth, seeking assistance from the sun god. His Pythia, a priestess who spoke for Apollo in a trance, declared that Zeus, king of all the gods, had transformed himself into the white bull in order to steal Europa, who would be none the worse for her experience. Cadmus had to give up the chase, but his coming to Delphi had been part of a higher destiny. The Pythia told him to find a black cow with a white crescent-moon design on its flank and follow the animal. Wherever the cow lay down, there the Phoenician was to found a new kingdom of great glory.

After leaving the oracle, Cadmus did indeed find a black cow with a white crescent figure on its flank. Alone, he followed it across Greece for many days until it finally lay down in a fertile though sparsely populated plain. He named his new country Boeotia, or Land of the Cow.

Lovely as the surroundings were, he could find no fresh water. The few natives, all poor wretches, gathered around him and said others had tried to make a kingdom of Boeotia before him but had failed because they could not overcome a terrible snake that guarded the solitary source of fresh water in the country. Only if Cadmus could defeat this monster would they acknowledge his kingship.

Taking his spear and shield, Cadmus set out to conquer the serpent. He lost his way in the unfamiliar land at night, and so he prayed to Artemis, goddess of the moon, Apollo's sister, to guide him. In the morning, a large rabbit Cadmus pursued as potential breakfast led him straight to a tall, conical pyramid made of round, undressed stones piled up to a sharp point. A large natural spring of fresh water bubbled close by.

His thrown spear felled the hare, but its cries awoke the gigantic, serpentine guardian that slept within the pyramid. It uncoiled from its strange lair and warned the Phoenician trespasser to return home at once. Instead, Cadmus ordered the serpent-guardian to leave the freshwater spring.

Sixth-century-B.C vase painting (Athens Archaeological Museum) of the conical stone pyramid protected by the "serpent guardian." Cadmus would kill the serpent, then sail off to the Blessed Islands of the far west.

"Depart or die!" hissed the monster. With that, Cadmus hurled his spear. The snake caught the lance in its jaws and snapped it in two.

The creature reared its head and struck with bared fangs at Cadmus, who raised his shield just in time to save himself. Desperate for a weapon, he pulled a loose stone from the conical pyramid and hurled it with all his strength at the head of the monster, which suddenly fell prostrate and mortally wounded at his feet.

"You are king now," the creature said weakly. "I am the last of the Serpent People. My race died out long ago. We were the first to settle this land, and I was commanded to protect our sacred spring from all intruders. Long have I fulfilled my duty. Now it is over. You fought bravely and cunningly, however, so you will make a good king. Grant me one last wish and I will bless you."

Cadmus promised to do whatever the guardian asked.

"After I am dead, heap up a mound of earth over my body. Do the same for the hare you killed. This will be an offering to Artemis and a memorial of this day and of my loyalty unto death. In return, remove my fangs and plant them in the earth. They will sprout into a new race from the old."

With a final hiss, the great serpent died.

Cadmus raised a mound over the monster near the cone-shaped pyramid and its freshwater spring, placing the hare under another mound nearby. He then sowed the guardian's fangs in the earth. Springing up in their place was a company of armored soldiers, who followed his orders implicitly.

Under his direction, they dismantled the conical structure and used its stones to build a citadel known as the Cadmea. He made the freshwater spring available freely to all, and Boeotia prospered, with Thebes as it capital and the Cadmea as his palace. He also taught his people how to read and write. He married a beautiful lady, Harmonia, who bore him many noble sons and lovely daughters.

After a long reign of greatness, Cadmus and his queen were both dying of old age, when they were suddenly transformed into serpents. The pair left Boeotia and swam across the seas into the distant west, until they arrived in the Isles of the Blessed. There they lived on as monarchs over a new kingdom, raising numerous royal children. In thanks to the spirit of the Serpent People for a rejuvenated life, Cadmus erected a tall, conical pyramid of round, undressed stones, similar to the structure defended by the snake-guardian he had killed many years before. Together with Harmonia, he lived on to reign as the gentle king of the Fortunate Isles.

The Cadmus myth has long been regarded by scholars as among the most historically valid of the ancient Greek stories.[1] For example, the Cadmea, or citadel, made from the stones of the serpent-guardian's rocky cone, was no literary invention. Northwest of Athens, it has been thoroughly excavated and dated to the early Bronze Age. Archaeological evidence at the site indicates the Cadmea was, in fact, a magnificent palace and the Theban capital of a state that rivaled Argolis as the center of Mycenaean power. Moreover, the Greek alphabet did indeed originate in Phoenician letters (our word "phonics" derives from "Phoenicia"), just as the Phoenician prince was supposed to have brought literacy to the early Greeks.

Even the cow that led Cadmus, who named his new kingdom after the wandering bovine, is rooted in reality. The Romans adopted a practice from Greece they called the *Italic ver sacrum,* or "sacred spring," again paralleling the natural spring appearing in the Cadmus myth. This was a means of dealing with overpopulation, wherein an ox or a cow with significant or unusual markings was allowed to wander freely, followed by the leader of a large contingent of settlers. Wherever the animal lay down, they established a new kingdom, which was henceforward referred to as a Bovianum, or "Ox Town." As John Pinsent explains, "One of the Greek tribes that came to Thebes seems to have followed the same custom, and it is the cow which has led to the association with Europa."[2]

But it is Cadmus's historical-mythic relationship to the lost civilization of Rock Lake that is most compelling. Foremost among its intriguing parallels with ancient Wisconsin is the conical pyramid made of piled, undressed stones inhabited by a serpent. With the very few exceptions mentioned below, no such structure was ever known to exist outside Rock Lake and the Canary Islands (not forgetting the vanished examples that once dotted the landscape from Rock Lake to the mining region of the Upper Peninsula). The Canaries were known in classical times as the Isles of the Blessed or the Fortunate Isles, the distant western realm in which Cadmus was supposed to have erected his cone-shaped memorial, and where, in fact, a twenty-foot tall, cone-shaped pyramid may still be seen near the shore of Lanzarote, in the modern capital of Arrecefe. Here, too, as we have learned, the native Canari or Guanches maintained kingdoms.

Details of the Cadmus myth draw an Old World connection to pre-Columbian Wisconsin much closer. The serpent-guardian's conical pyramid stood beside a water source, just as the cone-shaped structures at the bottom of Rock Lake stand near natural springs. A gravel and similarly conical mound behind the former walls of Aztalan also stood close to that site's freshwater spring.

Rude stone piles resembling cone-shaped pyramids, although much smaller than the pyramidal structures in Rock Lake and the Canary Islands, were built by several preclassical peoples in Europe and the Near East as markers over freshwater springs. Among the best known example is the Old Testament story of the Gigel (literally, "a heap"), a conical pile of stones taken from the River Jordan by the Hebrews to mark the precise spot where they crossed over into the Promised Land.[3] So, too, the stones used to build the Rock Lake structures were retrieved from a riverbed. Among the more obscure, fragmented references in the lesser known preclassical civilizations of Asia Minor, cone-shaped, stone pyramids were associated with the sun and stars, recalling the known astronomical alignments of Aztalan's conical mounds.[4]

These cogent parallels underscore the overseas connection to prehistoric Wisconsin, not necessarily with societies in the Near East or Asia Minor, but to a cultural theme that ran through the preclassical World. Their depictions in the Old Testament and the surviving records of ancient Anatolia, in Asia Minor, demonstrate that the cone-shaped pyramids functioned on several levels simultaneously: as tombs, observatories, indicators of freshwater springs and monuments.

All these purposes metaphysically combine to honor the spirits of the departed with water (a universal symbol of life), to trace the recurring motions of the heavenly bodies (another universal affirmation of immortality) and to memorialize some significant event associated with the deceased. Remarkably, all these functions associated with cone-shaped pyramids in the European ancient world and in the story of Cadmus perfectly coincide with everything understood about the conical structures under Rock Lake and on dry land in nearby Aztalan.

Even more remarkable parallels to his myth appear in the earth effigy mounds just south of Rock Lake and adjoining it, in a swampy area known as Mud Lake. They portray a four-thousand-foot-long snake staring at a rabbit, the same two animals featured in the Cadmus myth. The serpentine geoglyph of Lake Mills is the largest on earth. But it will be remembered that the monstrous guardian of the pyramidal cone asked Cadmus to heap a mound of earth over his corpse. The rabbit that led Cadmus to the snake's lair was a guide sent to help him after he prayed for assistance from Artemis, the moon goddess. The Mud Lake rabbit effigy's position as a lunar symbol is identified by the crescent moon-mound adjacent to it.

In Mesoamerica, the hare was a companion and messenger of the goddess of the moon, Ixchel to the Mayas and Coyolxauqui to the Aztecs. The rabbit, too, was buried beneath an earth mound by Cadmus, an offering to the serpent, just as it appears at Mud Lake. Of the more than ten thousand effigies within the cultural parameters of Aztalan Civilization—including Wisconsin, Upper Michigan, eastern Iowa and northern Illinois—the Mud Lake rabbit-mound is the only one of its kind and is, therefore, all the more significant in its apparent connection with the Cadmus myth. Only a very few snake effigies were known (one on the near-north side of Chicago that survived at least partially in somebody's backyard until World War I), but never in conjunction with a hare figure, again emphasizing the Mud Lake mounds' origins in ancient European themes.

Lunar symbols in the Cadmus myth additionally reflect the leading religious motif at Rock Lake, because that sacred body of water, according to surviving Native American testimony, was consecrated to the moon goddess. We recall Aztalan's Pyramid of the Moon and the crescent moon artifacts found near the lake. They recur in the white crescent moon on the black cow that led Cadmus to the site of his new kingdom, which he named after the animal, Boeotia. His dedication was made in the name of Artemis, the moon goddess, who sent the guiding bovine marked with her symbol: a crescent moon against its black hide representing the night sky.

A no less extraordinary parallel occurs in the relative dating of the Cadmus myth to the early Greek Bronze Age, around 1500 B.C., the same date assigned by hydrological studies to the pyramidal structures at the bottom of Rock Lake. Remarkable, too, is the Canary Island (Blessed Isles) connection linking Cadmus to the archaeological evidence at Lanzarote, suggesting the Atlantic origins of the Rock Lake civilizers.

The Phoenicians were famous as the foremost seamen of the ancient world. They circumnavigated the African continent two thousand years before Vasco de Gama and are known to have traveled to the Canary Islands in a flotilla commanded by one of their most capable admirals, Hanno.[5] But these expeditions took place centuries after the story of Cadmus was first told. Actually, the Phoenicians did not even exist as a people of any cultural significance until after the preclassical Bronze Age collapsed, around 1200 B.C. For the next five hundred years, Greece wallowed in a very real Dark Ages of terrible ignorance, relieved eventually by the coming of literacy from Phoenicia, just as the arrival of Cadmus, the Phoenician, implies. But his myth clearly deals with events in the earlier Bronze Age, not at the opening of classical times. Which people, then, did Cadmus actually represent, if not the Phoenicians?

In most oral traditions as old as his, certain elements get confused in the retelling, a deterioration of detail aggravated by the long Dark Ages through which it had to pass in Greece, until literacy was sufficiently restored to record the story in writing. It seems clear, then, that the "Phoenician" Cadmus who arrived by sea to conquer the native serpent-guardian and raise a new kingdom in Boeotia belonged to that same unknown prehistoric race that civilized Minoan Crete, Troy, Mycenaea and the rest of the Aegean World, beginning in the late fourth millennium B.C. Forgotten by the classical mythographers after the end of the Greek Dark Ages, they were assumed to have been Phoenicians for lack of any other known sea-people, and thus erroneously presented as such in the person of Cadmus. Indeed, his victory over the monster represents, not the coming of the Phoenicians, but the arrival of the same, far-earlier invaders who overthrew the resident old order.

The newcomers' takeover was exemplified in Apollo's struggle against Python, long regarded by scholars as the displacement of native power by outsiders. So too, Cadmus was directed by Apollo to defeat the snake-guardian, who himself proclaimed his identity as the last of the Serpent People. The Greeks always insisted that the race which came before them was the Pelasgian, or Sea Peoples, "born from the fangs of Ophion," the primeval serpent. Yet in the end, Cadmus and Harmonia were transformed into snakes, a strange fate for absolute foreigners. The implication, though, is that they are not entirely unrelated to the Serpent People of the guardian after all.

Cadmus appears to have belonged not to the historic Phoenicians but to the far more dimly remembered Pelasgians. Or, more precisely, to tribesmen, who, in their far-flung sea-rovings throughout the Mediterranean World over the centuries, became disassociated from the descendants of their own kinsmen, who themselves settled numerous, unaffiliated kingdoms in the Aegean and thus seemed almost like foreigners to one another.

A similar development took place during Roman times, when the Germanic peoples of Gaul and the Upper Rhine, although ancestrally bound to one another, split into many, divergent tribes with their own distinct identities. It is crucial to determine the people represented in the person of Cadmus, because they were most likely the original civilizers of Rock Lake, perhaps the first Europeans to cross the Atlantic Ocean, thousands of years before Columbus. They were the Pelasgian Sea People, earliest ancestors of the classical Greeks and the same culture-bearers better remembered as the Minoans, Trojans and Homer's Achaeans.

They voyaged far from their European homelands to obtain the mineral that fueled their Bronze Age, copper, which they found in sufficient abundance only at Michigan's Upper Peninsula and cleared through the mining town in Aztalan.

The visitors who today admire the tranquil beauty of Rock Lake do not suspect that 3,500 years ago, determined men in gleaming armor from the other side of the world stood at this same body of water. But what those men saw now lies hidden beneath the surface.

·15·

Aztalan, the Profaned Sacred Center

What cities, as great as this, have promised themselves immortality? Here stood their citadel, now grown over with weeds.
—Goldsmith

Most Midwesterners, even residents of Wisconsin, are surprised to learn that their Dairy State features its own authentically prehistoric pyramids. More properly known as temple-mounds, the two primary earthworks are part of Aztalan Archaeological Park, just south of I-94, some fifty miles west of Milwaukee. Visitors leave their cars in a lot beside a row of low, dome-shaped mounds, little more than unimpressive hillocks skirting a ridge. From them, the ground slopes gently eastward toward a line of trees concealing a tributary of the Rock River, the Crawfish. Beyond rolls a tranquil landscape of farmlands and pastures.

The first feature to catch the eye is an unusual high wall of wooden poles beginning in the direction of the river and running for about two hundred feet before turning at right angles for another fifty feet or so. This rough palisade is a very partial reconstruction made some thirty-five years ago to simulate the original fortification. A few posts have been slapped over with cement and wire mesh in crude imitation of the elegant mortar work that completely covered the original twelfth-century ramparts. Behind the walls stands a square earth mound, twenty feet across at its base and popularly known as the Pyramid of the Moon because of its lunar alignments. Looking south from its eleven-foot-high summit, visitors see the twenty-one-acre extent of the ancient enclosure, a low grassland with a fragmented construction of the recreated ramparts. Near the southwest corner stands the larger temple-mound known as the Pyramid of the Sun, since Dr. James Scherz confirmed its winter solstice alignments. A flight of broad, wooden stairs climbs up its western face to its fifteen-foot top, which provides the best perspective of Aztalan.

These scant remains only dimly and inadequately suggest the cultural splendor than once prevailed at this now peaceful place and leave modern visitors with scarcely an inkling of the human drama that occurred here. Thanks to the painstaking excavations and analytical research undertaken by surveyors and archaeologists since the 1830s, we know much about the real story of Aztalan, but many of its most important secrets have yet to be learned.

While views from atop the Pyramid of the Sun afford vistas of the whole site, they are misleading in some regards. What visitors see from this temple-mound anciently comprised only the innermost hub of a political state— a nation, perhaps—whose boundaries, still indefinitely known, could have stretched over most of what is now southern Wisconsin and into northern Illinois. Aztalan was the capital, citadel or ceremonial center of this vanished power, traces of which were left only in the effigy mounds (more than ten thousand of them) which once stretched from Chicago to the Upper Great Lakes, from the Mississippi River to Lake Michigan.

The partially reconstructed walls of Aztalan with its watchtowers.

Nor did the inhabitants dwell only behind the high walls of their capital. Settlement spread out intermittently, perhaps contiguously, from the ceremonial center to the shores of Rock Lake, only three miles to the west, and around Aztalan itself. The regional population might have risen as high as ten thousand residents. Certainly, a substantial laboring class resided in extended settlements just beyond and clustered around the imposing walls. As for the number of residents living within the enclosure, they probably numbered little more than a thousand; they were the elite, the royalty, astronomers, shamans, leading craftsmen, organizers and aristocracy of the land. Some idea of the importance of the persons living behind the walls is indicated by the 1,200 warriors necessary to man Aztalan's guard towers. In any case, the majority of people who were part of this Middle Mississippian culture center resided in the surrounding area and undoubtedly represented a figure several times greater than the privileged class within its protective battlements.

Also outside the fortification to the west rose a natural hill, terraformed by the ancient inhabitants to resemble a squat pyramid. It retains its shape to the present day. At its summit once stood an entirely man-made conical mound, sixty-five inches tall and thirty feet across at its base. It contained a pit thirty inches in diameter that went down four feet to two slabs of shaped catlinite. One was thirty by twenty inches and six inches thick; the other, six by fifteen inches and four inches thick. The purpose of their curious arrangement remained unknown for fifty years after their discovery until Dr. Scherz demonstrated the astronomical features of Aztalan. It is now understood that the four-foot-deep pit atop the pyramidal hill once contained a wooden post used to form celestial alignments with other points of reference. The two stone slabs were removable, allowing the post to be raised or lowered for different orientations. But its purpose was not purely scientific, at least not as we understand the term.

Catlinite was (and still is) the most sacred mineral on earth among all Native American tribes. The flesh-colored pipestone was named after George Catlin, the American painter who documented Native American life in the wild during the early nineteenth century. Catlinite, or pipestone, is not native to southern Wisconsin. The nearest deposits occur in Rice Lake, more than 220 airline miles northwest of Aztalan, so the stone was unquestionably an import. Pipestone was and is deemed especially holy because it is believed to be the flesh of an ancient humanity transformed after the Great Flood.

The presence of catlinite in this high mound implies that the hill possessed an extraordinary significance. Across the modern road from the farm on which the hill stands is the Greenwood Mound Group, five conical earth structures lining a ridge above the Aztalan enclosure.

They, too, possessed pits with stone walls at the bottom (although the walls were not of catlinite), flat platforms on which to raise or lower tall wooden

Aerial view of Aztalan in winter. Behind one of the partially reconstructed walls stand the Pyramid the Sun (bottom right) and Pyramid of Venus (top).

posts. These determined various celestial phenomena—lunar phases, solstices, stellar positions, etc. The terraformed hill with its own mound and pole was the focus of a central alignment which the Greenwood Group used in the manner of a gun sight to aim at desired astronomical targets; hence, its inclusion of pipestone, as though the ancient astronomers sought particular blessing for their efforts from the gods.

Long before Dr. Scherz's discovery of Pipestone Hill's archaeo-astromonical features, resident Indians preserved a recollection of its calendrical function in folklore. They told of the pinnacle grouse, a bird that flew in only one direction around the top of a conical hill. As it circled round and round, its plumage changed according to the season. Many Native Americans still associate the grouse with the sacred spiral of the heavens, the dance of the stars, while the bird symbolizes sky phenomena in general, particularly the motivating spirit of celestial events.[1]

The pinnacle grouse appears to represent the animus of seasonal change as it flies continuously in a circle (the cyclical movement of time) around the conical hill, the changing colors of its feathers corresponding to the alternating seasons marked by the post atop pipestone. In fact, Dr. Scherz demonstrated that the most significant astral alignments at Aztalan (the Pyramid of the Sun's orientations with Christmas Hill, across the Crawfish River) result in spiral coordinates. We are reminded, too, of the most common symbol recovered from Aztalan artifacts: the spiral.

Between Pipestone Hill and the walls of Aztalan formerly sprawled a ridge-top mound resembling an elongated pyramid, 150 feet long, 18 feet wide at the base, and 9 feet high. The tent-shaped feature ran on a north-south axis, its southern end configured into a triangle, with the northern terminus tapered to a point. Although made of earth and covered with a cap of painted clay, the mound's similarity to stone structures found at the bottom of Rock Lake is worth noting. By the 1930s, only a dim outline of the unusual earthwork bore witness to its former existence.

In the close vicinity of Aztalan were the effigy mounds of animals, identifiable objects and curious designs, many of colossal proportions and all sculpted from the earth with a stylized finesse and sophistication of technique precisely opposite to primitive.

Many of the effigies reflected a sea- or water-motif, such as a turtle mound near the east bank of the Crawfish River, directly across from the enclosure, or a 126-foot-long oar running parallel to the south end of the outermost wall. These lively geoglyphs appear to have had astronomical significance as well. Dr. Scherz showed that the turtle mound played an important role in creating alignments for the winter solstice. The immediate area swarmed with effigies of many shapes and sizes, more than seventy altogether, of which only a tiny handful still survive. But in their heyday, they must have imparted a very special atmosphere of living magic to the ceremonial center.

Aztalan's Pyramid of the Sun in autumn.

It was these writhing earth images that a thirteenth-century visitor to Aztalan would have encountered as he walked among the surrounding habitations of workers and artisans, traders and weavers, skinners and hunters, all in a hubbub of activity. But such scenes were certainly dominated by the sixteen-foot-high walls that ran for more than a mile around and through the entire complex. Their pastel white surfaces presented a solidly uniform exterior, because some two thousand gallons of lime plaster coated and completely covered the stockade of eleven thousand logs. Stones were used to reinforce gaps between some of them and in their foundations, where the ground was occasionally marshy. The high walls also possessed a unique, unusual feature, whose purpose is not definitely understood. Very large cauldrons or vats of fired clay pottery were stationed at intervals along the very top of the parapets. Perhaps they contained cane or some other flammable material and were used as fire beacons, as part of a ceremonial drama.

Standing four feet higher than the walls, 150 guard towers, spaced apart every fifteen feet, gave Aztalan a proud, Trojan appearance. The square towers were provided with long, narrow windows from which archers could set up a withering crossfire on a besieging attacker with maximum protection.

But Aztalan had no gates, no doors of any kind, yet people could pass through the walls with ease, if they knew the secret. An entrance was cleverly concealed by one section of the wall slightly overlapping the next section just behind it, creating an open, narrow space easily guarded from within while allowing access for only one person at a time. From even a short distance in front of the wall, the entrance could not be detected.

Beyond the walls, near the south end of the enclosure, rests a large, somewhat oblong boulder, about one and a quarter tons, and the only one of its kind at the site. When the recreated fortifications were being built in the 1950s, the big stone was moved by a bull-dozer from its original position because it "got in the way," to quote one of the workers. Thirty years later, Dr. Scherz discovered its original location by determining its role as an alignment marker for astronomical observations from the top of the Pyramid of the Sun.

The stone is particularly provocative, because the only other monoliths known to orient with important sky phenomena are the menhirs of Neolithic Europe. Similar megalithic alignments still exist along America's eastern seaboard (Mystery Hill being the most famous), and the old-European character of these structures likewise seems certain. But the Aztalan monolith is special, because it and the stone circle at Goose Island, also three miles away from Rock Lake, in the west, are the only such features west of the Alleghenies.

Not far from the toppled menhir's present position was a stone aqueduct that originally ran a great distance from east to west. When surveyed in the 1850s, little of it survived as testimony to the irrigation skills of the prehistoric inhabitants. Speculation has been rife ever since that the ancient

This fallen monolith once served as a standing reference to calculate celestial alignments for astronomer-priests in their observatory-temple atop Aztalan's Pyramid of the Sun, in background.

aqueduct actually connected Aztalan with Rock Lake, a phenomenal achievement for the pre-Columbian engineers.

Once inside the walls, our thirteenth-century visitor would have been astounded by the enclosure's contrast with the outside world. The foremost attraction was the Pyramid of the Sun near the southwest corner of the site. Seventy-one feet square at the base, it was a step-pyramid rising in two layers and completely encased in a smoothed, bright-yellow clay cap. No mere heap of dirt, it was a skillful arrangement of gravel, red and white sand, mottled black earth, river mud and fire-hardened clay—all constructed to hold the pyramid's shape through centuries of erosional forces.

The exterior of the temple-mound was profusely decorated with geometric designs in which spirals predominated, painted in dark-blue pigments extracted from vegetable fibers. A broad flight of wooden stairs rose from its base to the summit, which was crowded by an observatory shrine. Its walls were white stucco, and the very steep roof rose another sixteen feet over the whole structure. Protruding even higher through the roof of dried prairie grass was a lofty, red-painted cedar pole anchored at the center of the building and into the top of the mound. Two doorways opened to the east and the west, accommodating the sun god's appearances in his risings and settings. From this privileged spot, the entire precinct could be surveyed at a glance.

Two more walls bisected the enclosure, providing the residents with an even more effective defense. The trees which today line the river banks and grow inside the archaeological zone would have been absent during Aztalan's greatness, when they were felled for timber. Opposite the Pyramid of the Sun, to the east, was a natural knoll of gravel near a freshwater spring that supplied the community. Certainly, this feature played some ceremonial role and may have contributed to the location's choice as a sacred center.

Running north of the knoll, parallel to the river bank, was the residential area. It had no streets as such, the houses only casually arranged without regard to city planning of any kind. There were two types of domiciles:

the wall trench and the single-post construction. In the former, a trench was dug around a spiral pattern in which posts were sunk and the house developed. Single-post structures had their posts planted in the ground upon which the house was raised. Both kinds were mortared in wattle and daub, a combination of moist clays and plant fibers. Fire was then applied to create a strong insulation known as "Aztalan brick."

As a further defense against the harsh winters, all the homes were oriented with their backs to the cold northwest winds. Roofs were made of thatch, each pierced by a smoke-hole to allow ventilation for a central hearth, around which were pole-frame suspension beds covered with bear furs and deer skins. Each house was a single-family dwelling for mother, father, three or four children and sometimes grandparents. Evidence of regularly swept floors shows the ancient inhabitants were fastidious housekeepers, and some homes featured brick fire-boxes that served as both heaters and ovens.

Nearby were storage pits containing nuts, seeds, maize, choke-cherries and berries. Meat was stored outside and included raccoon, buffalo, moose, muskrat, squirrel, beaver, rabbit, bear, deer and elk. Favorite fowl included pigeons, swans, quail, ducks, reedbirds, geese, turkeys and teals. Hunting took place in a vast oak forest that stood across the river, and most game birds were found in marshes to the east and north.

The inhabitants of Aztalan also consumed great quantities of pickerel, pike, perch, bullhead, catfish, bass, drum, gar, buffalo fish and suckers. Freshwater clams were likewise in demand. Large-scale harvests were effected in actual fish factories or stone weirs just beneath the surface of the Crawfish River, into which catches were driven and corralled. Remnants of at least one such factory may still be seen about a quarter of the mile south of the ceremonial center.

Much of their food was processed for prolonged storage in large clay vats, while most of it was brought in as trade by Plains Indians from all over the southern Wisconsin area.

In the northeast section of the site was another square mound. Atop it stood a temple forty by ninety feet at the base. It housed ritual fire pits lined with white sand, perhaps imported from the Florida Gulf Coast specifically for cult purposes. After each ceremonial conflagration, the pits were refilled with the special white sand. The mound's counterpart in the northwest section is commonly known as the Pyramid of the Moon for its lunar alignments. It originally stood nine feet high and measured one hundred five feet in length and more than eighty feet in width. The top was sixty by forty feet and featured a crematorium twelve feet long by five feet wide on the west side of the mound.

Arranged in a southwest-northeast orientation, the five-foot-tall structure covered a two-foot-deep trench lined with a large mat of woven cattail rushes. Into this pit the human remains of ten adults, male and female, were laid in a row on their backs in extended positions. The log structure and its interred dead were then ritually burned to ashes. Much later, an eleventh burial of human bones wrapped in a bundle was included. After the fire ran its course, another and final level of the mound was heaped over the crematorium.

While there is no physical evidence for a temple building atop the Pyramid of the Moon, its absence would certainly have been out of character with the other two earth mounds, which both featured sacred structures, so most investigators assume the northwest pyramid did indeed have its own temple similar to the others. And, like the others, the mound was probably capped by a hard layer of smoothed clay decorated with geometric designs.

Between the Pyramid of the Moon and that of the Sun was a broad, open area or plaza for public assemblies and sports events, such as ritual ball games, which symbolically simulated the movements of the sun and moon (appropriately enough). Midway between the two mounds and abutting the plaza was a broad ramp of earth and posts that sloped to the top of the walls, presumably to allow large numbers of defenders to man their stations in the shortest possible time.

At the center of the south end of the enclosure was a large pool of clear water shaped in a triangular configuration. As Increase Lapham, the early nineteenth-century surveyor who saw the pool, remarked, "Perhaps the bottom may have been rendered water-tight by artificial means."[2] Its purpose may have been a great deal more significant than bathing and almost certainly served ritual purposes. The triangle-pool's apex pointed due north, toward a low-roofed, rectangular building stored with tons of raw, high-grade copper.

At the exact center of Aztalan was a pair of adult, human skulls, both upside-down, side by side and in a pit, precisely oriented east and west. "It seems hardly likely," wrote S. A. Barrett, the chief archaeologist who excavated the skulls in 1933, "that they were carelessly cast into this pit and fell accidentally in these positions. It seems more probable that they were purposely placed in these positions for some reason."[3] The skulls imply, however, that Aztalan was a sacred center, an implication reinforced by their east-west orientation, as symbolic of a spiritual crossroads or midpoint. This interpretation is reinforced by their discovery at the precise center of the enclosure.

While the two skulls and eleven other persons interred in the Pyramid of the Moon represent the only ritual burials behind Aztalan's walls, a few others took place in their shadow, just beyond the enclosure. A conical mound of gravel covered the bodies of two boys, one ten, the other five years old. Laid out full length on their backs, with their lower limbs slightly flexed, they were covered with the large carapace of a turtle that had been worked into some kind of dish or tray. The shell was imported from the Gulf of Mexico. Doubtless the children were somehow special, deemed worthy of a unique interment and may have been brothers who belonged to a privileged family, perhaps to the lord of Aztalan himself, and might therefore have been princes. Or they could have been sacrifices to consecrate Aztalan at its inception.

As Barrett wrote, "in every way the burial showed considerable age," conceivably going back to the foundation of the town.[4] Interestingly, boy-sacrifice, or the substitution of piglets for boys, occurred in Neolithic Europe to consecrate megalithic structures such as Stonehenge. The best known example takes place in the story of Merlin, when, as a youth, he was threatened with ritual execution to hallow a particular site.

While the boys buried at Aztalan may or may not have been princes, a "princess" was indeed discovered about three hundred feet north of the enclosure. So named after the extraordinary funeral garb of a young, adult woman found under an earthen conical mound originally six feet high and thirty feet across, hers was the most elaborate prehistoric grave ever excavated in North America above the Rio Grande. Belonging to a twenty-eight-year-old female, the corpse had been carefully wrapped in a full-length bark envelope, long since rotted away, and accompanied by numerous perishable objects, grave goods to honor the deceased, that only left faint, unintelligible traces in the soil. The woman was clothed in a fabulous gown hung with three woven belts of individually cut, brightly polished mother-of-pearl around her shoulders, waist and calves. The shell ornaments were pierced and strung, then tastefully arranged to taper in size from the largest to the smallest beads, beginning at the shoulders and hips and joining at center clasps. Some of the shells used in the production of her gown were imported from the Gulf of Mexico and all were separately fashioned into squares, rectangles or circles. Her necklace was comprised of 585 beads, 846 went into her belt, with 547 for the calf-belt. Altogether, 1,978 individual pieces were sewn into her garment. If this impressive raiment was not exclusively funereal and occasionally worn by the woman in life, she could have been counted upon for some spectacular personal appearances.

In any case, the Beaded Princess hints at the grandeur and drama that was long ago celebrated in Aztalan. An additional eighteen polished shell beads were tossed into her grave by mourners, as they buried her, behavior completely contrary to the burial customs of the Plains Indians.

The princess was herself a strange specimen. Her five-foot, seven-inch skeleton belonged to a woman unusually tall for most Native Americans of her sex. Normally, she would have stood almost six feet, but her spine was badly deformed. Obvious abnormalities often convinced tribal societies that such misshapen persons had been singled out by the gods for special powers and insights, qualifying them as religious leaders. Given the details of her burial, the princess was more likely a highly honored shaman.

Very few other graves have been found in the vicinity of Aztalan. One contained the remains of an exceptionally tall man. His corpse had originally been placed reverentially on a mat of woven reeds and accompanied by some simple grave goods, pottery and bags of acorns. These honored circumstances were in sharp contrast to the otherwise good condition of the body: it had been decapitated before interment.

Only three other graves covered by animal effigy mounds across the Crawfish River have been found. In fact, all graves in the Aztalan area seem to represent exclusive ritual burials. The cemetery used by the prehistoric residents has never been identified and how they disposed of their dead continues to mystify investigators. If cremation was the method of disposal, no evidence for it exists other than the remains of only eleven persons in the Pyramid of the Moon.

There are many enigmas in this strange place. When excavated, a ridge-top mound beyond the northern wall was found to contain a square chamber lined with walls of birch bark. It contained nothing but a 162-pound rock. When shown to Ho Chunk elders, they recoiled in horror from "the spirit stone" and offered no further explanation.[5] Another object dug up near the Pyramid of the Sun has never been explained. Made of highly polished chert, a very fine-grained, tough stone composed mainly of silica, it is a beautifully formed, almost perfect square. The four sides measure thirty-eight, thirty-seven, thirty-eight, and forty millimeters, and it is five millimeters thick. A great deal of precision work went into creating the object, whatever its purpose.

Only scraps remain of the colorful textiles manufactured by the ancient inhabitants for clothing, and few of their personal ornaments have been recovered. One prize find is a triangular pendant of copper.

More of their tools still exist, and these include finely made axes, hammers, chisels, drills, spades and levers—all testimony to a creative, industrious people. They were ingenious workers in natural materials, as exampled in the hoes they made from milkstone, which not only conformed perfectly for use as a tool, but, whenever damaged, always fractured along lines that kept its shape.

Milkstone is not native to Wisconsin and must have been brought in from Illinois. The people of Aztalan operated a trading network that stretched for thousands of miles in each direction, largely for the importation of shells for ornamentation or religious practices, such as the turtle carapace from the Gulf of Mexico used as a grave good in the boys' burial. Some of these imported mollusk shells included specimens from Georgia's Atlantic coast; Key West, Florida; the West Indies; the Ohio Valley; Central America; and Cape Cod. They employed the Florida conch, penultimately the largest in the Gulf Region and used by the civilizers of Aztalan and Mesoamerican ceremonial centers alike as a trumpet. Many of these luxury goods were brought to Aztalan from great distances in exchange for calendrical information provided by the astronomers, who could tell farmers when to plant or harvest what crops at the optimum time, or give them a timetable for some particular ritual activity meant to win favor from the gods.

Near the inner bank, at the south end of the site, the outermost wall actually extended out into the onrushing Crawfish River, thereby including a portion of the stream within the village confines, where it was used for purposes of irrigation. Close by this extension was a spring of fresh water twenty-two feet long and ten feet wide, carefully paved with flat stones that ran in a line into the compound. Both here and at the site of another spring a mile north of Aztalan, the pavement stones were laid out into the water itself.

Virtually nothing is known about the physical appearance of the people of Aztalan, save that they were regarded as "foreigners" by the Ho Chunk and as "white men" by the Menomonie.[6] At least a certain strata of their population practiced skull-elongation, in which infants had their heads strapped between two cloth-covered boards. After the first year of growth, the head was sufficiently deformed, probably for aesthetic reasons, which likewise indicates the existence of a social upper class.

Aztalan was far more than a settlement, however. It was a mining town, through which flowed enormous quantities of raw copper shipped down from the Upper Great Lakes. The miners wintered in Aztalan, planted their crops in the spring, traveled to work Michigan's copper mines during the summer and returned to harvest their crops in the fall. To regulate all these vital activities, which were strictly circumscribed by the seasons, an accurate and reliable conception of time was imperative. To this end, numerous, even redundant, solar, lunar and stellar alignments were calculated, and the temple-mounds became points of reference from which multiple celestial phenomena could be studied simultaneously.

The Greenwood Group of dome-shaped mounds with their adjustable center posts "ranged themselves along the sky-line," as solstices, eclipses, phases, equinoxes, astral cycles, Venusian recurrences, constellations in position and all manner of heavenly data accumulated behind the high walls of the sacred center.[7] People traveled great distances to learn what to do for their crops, when to risk a journey by water, when to marry or relocate. In exchange for such critically important information, they brought goods from throughout and far beyond the Mississippi valley.

Aztalan's astronomer-priests obtained latitude measurements using the North Star and figured the declination of the sun (23.5 degrees). Mud Lake's rabbit mound, whose parallel lunar symbolism in Maya and European Bronze Age myths has been examined previously, was positioned to look at a conjunction of the new moon and a trio of planets, while the nearby snake effigy marked sunrise at the winter solstice.

These and abundant additional observations did not develop overnight in Aztalan. Astronomy and all the other skills of government, pyramid building, agriculture, irrigation and social organization arrived suddenly and fully evolved in southern Wisconsin around A.D. 1100. And for two hundred years, the people of Aztalan flourished while their fame spread throughout the Middle Mississippian culture of which they were the leading exponents.

But sometime before their bicentennial, a segment of their society degenerated into the horrors of a death cult. Evidence has been recovered of more than eight hundred persons cannibalized behind the walls of Aztalan toward the close of its existence. Doubtless many more grizzly remains still lie under the blood-soaked grounds of the enclosure. Discovered in the kitchen middens, together with turkey bones and bear claws, were human femurs cracked open to remove the edible marrow. Whether the abominable practice was confined to some ritualizing group or contributed to an internal schism that brought society to an end is uncertain. But reliable, abundant carbon-dating confirms that Aztalan was suddenly consumed in a single, massive conflagration that reduced the entire site to cinders. The once prosperous ceremonial center must have burned for days, illuminating the surrounding area with its cataclysm and turning the Catfish River that flowed by its blazing walls into a torrent of garishly reflected flame.

For the next five hundred years, its charred ruins were forsaken by local Plains Indians, who shunned dead Aztalan as profaned ground. Thus ended the strange story of a mysterious people and their ancient city in Wisconsin. But memory of them would continue to haunt their sacred lake to the present day.

·16·

Tyranena, Sunken City of the Dead

So many great nobles, kings, administrators, so many brave nations, so many proud princes, and power so splendid—in a moment, a twinkling, all utterly ended!

—Jacopane

Discoveries made beneath Rock Lake, anciently known as Tyranena, share many similarities with comparable features excavated in Aztalan. The prehistoric settlement is, after all, only three miles east of the lake, so we do not assume too much when we speculate that the waters were familiar to Wisconsin's pre-Columbian inhabitants.

More pertinent to our subsurface quest, parallels between Aztalan and finds made under Rock Lake lend credibility to the existence of a ruined civilization lying at its bottom. Among the most obvious and valid of those parallels begins with the one hundred-foot-long structure discovered by sonar in 1989. Since known as the Limnatis pyramid, it is a tent-like stone mound sixty feet down and oriented along a north-south axis at the edge of the lake's oldest former shoreline.

Until its destruction before 1930, a ridge-top mound virtually identical to its sunken counterpart, save only that it was made of earth and clay, lay in the shadow of Aztalan's western wall. Additionally, running parallel to the underwater mound along the lake's modern eastern shoreline and lying identically on a north-south axis was an earth mound 135 feet long and entirely comparable to the Limnatis pyramid. Obviously, ridge-top mound-building continued in an unbroken chain of monumental construction from the land to what is now the bottom of Rock Lake, since structures identical in design and size appear both around the lake and beneath it.

The divers of Michael Kutska's group in 1968, like Richard Boyd's underwater expedition a few years later, uncovered caches of mollusk shells in two separate ridge-top buildings at the bottom of Rock Lake. On dry land, at the south shore of the lake, a conical earth mound five feet tall and ten feet across at the base, excavated around 1900, was found to contain a similar cache of clam shells stored as grave goods in a human burial of ashes, bones and skulls.

The ancient inhabitants of Aztalan went to great lengths to import specially sought-after mollusks for ornamental and ritual purposes from as far away as the Atlantic seaboard, the Florida Gulf Coast and the West Indies. The most ornate burial in pre-Columbian America north of Mexico belonged to the so-called "Beaded Princess," entombed outside Aztalan's enclosure. Her splendid gown comprised nearly two thousand mother-of-pearl pendants handcrafted from mollusk shells. Clearly, shell was a valuable commodity that was at least partly associated with mortuary ceremonies, and today, as a revealing artifact, it draws illuminating comparisons between the burial structures around the shores of Rock Lake and on its bottom.

Representation of a stone structure found in the western quadrant of Rock Lake.
Model by Wayne May, on display in the Aztalan Museum

The mounds of the Greenwood Group just northwest of Aztalan's enclosure are more dome-shaped than conical, but their summits were pierced by deep shafts to accommodate alignment posts. So too, some of the conical structures found under the lake are hollow at the top. The subsurface pyramids are even lined up in a north-south row, like the Greenwood Group members. These earthworks enclosed a "cement-like cone of mixed clay and gravel," recalling Max Nohl's description of the cone-shaped pyramid he discovered, its round stones bonded by a kind of cement, under the south end of Rock Lake.[1] Perhaps dozens of similar conical structures once spread from Michigan's Upper Peninsula down into southern Wisconsin.

Rock Lake's two effigy mounds located by side-scan sonar in 1989 represent a continuation of the same geoglyphs that surrounded the lake shore and Aztalan itself. The sunken figures appear to be made of stone and are oriented almost precisely on an east-west axis, side by side. One is the image of a turtle stylized in the fashion of animal earth-sculpture common throughout pre-historic Wisconsin. Its companion depicts a headless man. Both are about six feet long and just as wide and lie eighteen feet beneath the surface.

The turtle effigy is exemplary proof that human activity did indeed take place many centuries ago on what has long since become the bottom of Rock Lake. This important piece of evidence is reinforced by the docu-mented previous existence of another earthen turtle mound that was located on dry land, the modern shoreline, and exactly parallel to the sunken effigy, until its destruction in the 1920s, when the boat landing and beach were installed. The underwater effigy was separated on a straight east-west line from its land-bound counterpart by one quarter of a mile.

Just across the Crawfish River from Aztalan lies a six-hundred-foot-long turtle mound aligned with features behind the enclosure to determine astronomical data. The locations of these figures, depicting as they do an aquatic animal near the banks of the Crawfish River, on the present coast of Rock Lake and at its prehistoric subsurface shoreline, all confirm the sig-nificance of their positions, as intended by their creators.

Beyond the west bank of the Crawfish, a pair of young boys were respect-fully entombed under a large turtle shell. The resident Plains Indians equated the turtle with cowardice, braggadocio, obscenity and human frailty, char-acteristics which would not make it eligible for memorialization as cere-monial mounds or as honored burial goods. The creature obviously meant something entirely different to the builders of Aztalan, a difference that apparently extended to their ethnic identity.

Because of its ability to survive in both water and on land, the prehistoric culture-bearers more likely regarded the turtle as a living symbol of spiritual transformation from earth to the afterlife, which finds its human archetype in water and especially among sacred lakes. Such an interpretation of the ani-mal's ancient significance is lent credence by the Crawfish River's colossal turtle mound, which is oriented 23.5° south of east, the declination of the

*Hopewell earthworks at Ohio's Mound City
closely resemble those found in Rock Lake.*

Photograph by Joseph Murray. Courtesy, National Park Service.

sun north of the equator at the solstices. The solstices are universally regarded in higher cultures as the most dramatic moments of seasonal change, paralleling human birth, life, death and rebirth. The inclusion of a specially imported turtle shell to serve as a spiritually valuable grave good in the burial of the two Aztalan boys reaffirms the animal's identity as a symbol of transition from worldly existence to the afterlife. In any case, the turtle mounds stretching from underwater to the land graphically trace a common cultural pattern running unbroken from the bottom of Rock Lake to Aztalan itself.

The headless-man mound is no less significant. It is unique among Wisconsin effigies, save for one other example on land. But three miles due east, in the immediate vicinity of Aztalan, north of its enclosure, lay the grave of a male skeleton minus a skull. Everything about the burial suggested an honored, ritualized interment, just as the headless figure in the lake probably signified a mystery religion related to the so-called "Southern Death

Cult" that was associated with the mound-builders and flourished until the fourteenth century throughout the Mississippi valley.

The position of Rock Lake's headless-man mound directly adjacent to the turtle effigy, symbol of the soul's transition from physical existence to the spirit realm, could not be more appropriate. Together with the other turtle mound facing them on shore, they almost formed a kind of hieroglyph we may read thusly: The turtle (soul) on land (the physical world) moves into the waters of transformation, where death (the headless-man effigy) makes the transition to new life (the subsurface turtle mound). The three figures combine to identify Rock Lake as a sacred center, where rites of a mystery religion dedicated to principles of an afterlife were celebrated.

The effigies likewise define the lake as a necropolis, a city of the dead, where the pyramid forms were heaped up as memorials to persons of distinction. Aztalan's elaborate grave sites—the Beaded Princess, the headless man, the two princes, etc.—extended directly from the mortuary magnificence of Rock Lake's stone monuments.

It was among those conical, donut-shaped and ridge-top structures and the honored dead they entombed that the rites and ceremonies of a rebirth cult occurred with all the colorful pageantry suggested in the material magnificence of Aztalan.

The ancient cemetery of Aztalan has never been identified. Only fifteen or so burials were found in and around the enclosure, and those were exclusively of a ritualized character. Investigators need look no further for that cemetery than Rock Lake. More than seventy known burial mounds surrounded its shores until the early twentieth century. They contained human bones and ashes, evidencing both inhumation and cremation, the same dual funeral practices which took place in Aztalan.

The Wisconsin Archaeologist reported that "many skeletons were taken from mounds at Rock Lake and forwarded to the U.S. Army Medical Museum."[2] A very large mound, possibly a natural hill, formerly occupied

*Mid-nineteenth-century illustration of conical stone mounds
(identical to examples being discovered in Rock Lake) found
and almost entirely dismantled by early European settlers.*

a position at the south end of the lake. As it was being demolished to make
way for a railroad trestle, many hundreds, probably thousands of human
bones were uncovered and removed. The same issue of *The Wisconsin Archaeologist* described these coastal burial mounds as conical and linear, the identical configurations spotted by divers in the lake. And, like the sunken
ridge-top stone structures, their correspondents on dry land were aligned
in a north-south direction. Even their dimensions (135 feet long, 8 feet tall,
and 20 feet wide) compare very closely to the underwater monuments.

It seems clear, then, that Aztalan's missing cemetery is Rock Lake, both
along its shores and beneath its waves. Indeed, the apparent symbolism of
its turtle and headless-man mounds strongly imply its identity as a sacred
necropolis. The material evidence of the land, stretching from Aztalan to the
edge of the lake, overlaps the subsurface evidence so precisely that no other
conclusion seems possible.

As though additional conformation were necessary, an effigy mound described by *The Wisconsin Archaeologist* as "a water spirit form" used to lie eighty-four feet along the south shore of Rock Lake, near the large burial hill.[3] Before it, too, was obliterated, its erect head was ten feet wide rising from a twenty-four-foot-long body with a sixty-foot-long tail. Front and rear limbs were fifteen feet across. Its enormous size and appropriate symbolism as "a water spirit" clearly demonstrated the holy regard in which the prehistoric residents held the lake as a sanctified resting place for their dead. Both their effigy mounds and various types of monumental structures formed an unbroken line from the land into the lake.

But the closest underwater comparison with Aztalan is the Great Triangle in the middle of Rock Lake's south end. The delta-shaped formation may be a mound, although its construction materials, whether clay or stone, are unknown. It nonetheless constitutes some of the best evidence for Wisconsin's sunken civilization.

During its prehistoric prime, Aztalan's walls enclosed a large pool configured into a triangle. Like its far greater Rock Lake counterpart, it was located in the middle of the south end of the site with its apex pointed due north. Both may have been constructed together at the same time to establish some mystical correspondence between the lake and the ceremonial center. The Tyranena delta-mound was possibly a sacred pool, the same function observed in Aztalan's triangle. Their esoteric relationship suggests a sharing of common elements linking the lake to the settlement, thereby confirming both as actually two aspects of a single, common sacred center belonging simultaneously to the water and the land, rather than separate places unrelated to each other.

The Rock Lake and Aztalan delta formations are duplicated at only one other location on earth, in coastal Peru, among the famous Nazca lines.

Created by clearing away surface stones to expose the underlying sand, the drawings include recognizable zoomorphic shapes and abstract geometrical designs. Among the latter is a three-hundred-foot-long triangle. Like its Wisconsin counterparts, its apex points due north. It is difficult to dismiss the widely separated sites as the fortuitous coincidence of wholly unrelated peoples, because the Ecuadoran Canari had intense commercial relations with both coastal Peru, where Chincha, their capital city, was located, and Rock Lake-Aztalan. So too, Aztalan had trade connections at least as far south as Central America. The Peruvian parallel with prehistoric Wisconsin underscores arguments on behalf of the Aztalaners as far-ranging copper barons with vital links throughout the Americas.

The implication of the cult-turtle, at once embodying the water-world and the land-world, seems all the more valid and applicable to the spiritual symbolism apparently at work here.

There are additional comparisons forging Aztalan's profound link with Rock Lake. The Ho Chunk preserve a tribal memory of ancient days, when shamans of "the foreign chiefs" pretended to walk across the surface of the lake at night, carrying torches in their outstretched hands. Seeking to deceive and overawe the common people, the shamans were said to have accomplished the trick by walking on stepping stones placed just below the surface.[4] The same performances may have taken place in Aztalan, where pavement running out into and just beneath the surface of a fresh spring pool were detected by archaeologists in the 1930s.

Similarly paved arrangements were found a mile or so north of Aztalan, on the same bank of the Crawfish River. These discoveries tended to validate the Native American tradition and establish another revealing connection between alleged activities at Aztalan and Rock Lake, where the water-walking show probably occurred along the top of a linear mound lying inches below the surface.

But the larger features, such as the one-hundred-foot-long Limnatis pyramid, would still have been under forty feet of water. They sit on the edge of the lake's oldest shoreline, which dates back to before 1500 B.C., and were undoubtedly constructed by the area's first civilizers. It was the copper miners who raised the colossal monuments, using stones from a nearby river and other concretions left by the retreating glacier that carved out Rock Lake five thousand years before.

Even centuries after their sudden departure in 1200 B.C., the site they abandoned was regarded throughout the Middle West and probably beyond as a particularly venerable sacred center. Over time, it took on mythic proportions in the minds of generations of Native Americans; Rock Lake was by no means unknown to the culture bearers who decided upon a location for Aztalan just east of the lake. On the contrary, its fame certainly played a major role in their selection of the banks of the Crawfish. The river at that time (A.D. 1100) better facilitated ship traffic, because the waterway systems had shifted away from Rock Lake in the more than two millennia since its role in the ancient copper trade. Perhaps the structures under the lake were built by two different peoples living at two distinct periods of time, separated by more than two thousand years, but united in the enduring sacredness of the place they chose for their population center.

·17·

An Update to
the 1992 Edition

"Never utter these words: 'I do not know this, therefore, it is false.' One must study to know, know to understand, understand to judge."

The Hindu *Apothegm of Narada*

On April 27, 2001, six men and two women boarded a pair of small open boats, and steered for an area approximately fifty feet from the eastern shore, off Fremont Street. During a fly-over the previous year, aerial observers noticed two peculiar black spots in Rock Lake. At three thousand feet, they were only dots on the otherwise muddy brown bottom, but suggested possible man-made objects that merited closer inspection.

When we reached the suspected area, we began a visual search, and almost at once our fourteen-year-old deck hand yelled out that he saw a dark shape under water not far ahead. In moments, we were drifting over a mysterious shadow not far beneath our hull. Video-cameraman Steven Dahl and I quickly struggled into our scuba gear, then threw ourselves over the side. The cold water was a shock to experience, but my shivering skin eventually adjusted to the fifty-degree temperatures. Steve was better equipped in a dry suit. My body heat took time to warm up the thin layer of water the wet suit allowed to circulate around me. Subsurface visibility, about fifteen feet, was uncommonly good for Rock Lake, and we had the luxury of beholding the target in its entirety. It was unquestionably man-made, its top less than six feet beneath the waves. Dark gray slabs had been formed into a stone mound approximately six feet high and nine feet long from north to south, and seven feet wide.

Everything about it resembled a monumental grave typical of the Adena. These were a Paleolithic people who built numerous stone structures throughout North America's upper Midwest three thousand years ago. Some scholars regard the Adena as the continent's first civilized race. The mound was nicely made, not very ruinous. Its oval configuration complemented its probable function as a tomb, signifying the human soul's rebirth from the cosmic egg, a spiritual concept understood by many high cultures around the world before the onset of Christianity. In any case, the structure's location matched its position as determined by our aerial reconnaissance.

After recording its precise coordinates and completing our underwater photography, we returned to shore, not entirely convinced that the mound was ancient, despite all appearances. Perhaps it was a piling for a old pier from the early twentieth century. It seemed too good to be true.

Back at the motor home that Steve shared with his wife, Pattie, we reviewed his video. Although clearly shot, he had not pulled back far enough for the mound to be seen in its entirety, resulting in images resembling only a disorganized rock pile. Moreover, my borrowed underwater camera had jammed, preventing me from taking any photographs, so we all agreed to return to the site the next morning. By then, winds had picked up dramatically, whipping the surface into whitecaps. By early afternoon, conditions improved at least enough for us to put our boats back in the water.

*Sonar image of the enormous delta structure at the south end of
Rock Lake shows its uniform sides. Stone mounds appear as spots.*
Courtesy Archie Eschborn, Rock Lake Research Society.
See web site http://www.rocklakeresearch.com

As we approached the target area, Capt. Michael Cushway, who was standing at the helm, called out that we just passed over *another* dark shape very similar in size to the Fremont Street mound. Aerial observers had indeed photographed two black spots in this vicinity. Steven and I splashed over the side again but were unable to see much. The previous day's water clarity, agitated by the high winds, had badly deteriorated. With directional help from Pattie, who kept one eye on the target and the other on our position, we finally found the dark shape.

Even in the reduced visibility, we could see that it was identical in virtually all respects to the Fremont Street mound. This time, my camera functioned, and Steve pulled back far enough for his video to take in the whole structure. Like the previous day's target, its loose slab-stones seemed to make for an unlikely piling. We returned to the dive boat, then relocated the Fremont Street structure, which we tried to photograph in Rock lake's typically poor visibility.

In the evening, I shared everything we had learned about our finds with Robert Dauffenbach, the Department of Natural Resources officer in residence at the lake, responsible for its care and knowledgeable about its history. He doubted that the stone mounds were the remains of an old pier, because their separation (about two hundred feet) and distance from shore was too great. Moreover, so far as he knew, no harbor facilities of any kind had ever been built in that section of the lake. Lloyd Hornbostel later pointed out that the mounds' obviously man-laid courses of stone precluded its modern origin, because water levels were not low enough to allow their construction in modern times. The underwater structures, in their opinion, were probably prehistoric man-made monuments, perhaps burial mounds, as we suspected.

We named the Fremont Street structure in honor of the sharp-eyed son of our captain, who made the discovery. Its companion, found the next day, was christened after his younger brother, because he was the first person

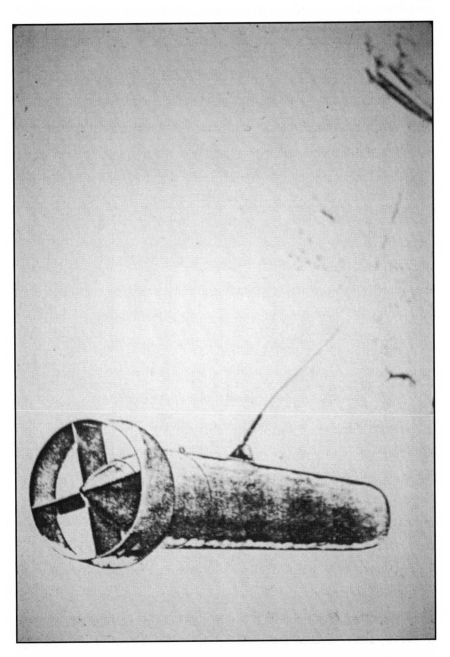

Illustration of the sonar torpedo pulled behind our research vessel.

known to swim out to it from shore. So Luke's Mound and Amos Mound are the latest secrets yielded up by that mysterious lake.

Others have come to light in the years following the first publication of *The Lost Pyramids of Rock Lake* in 1992. Among the most interesting was the discovery of another underwater effigy mound, this one resembling a serpent or dragon. Its location at the southern end paralleled the same bioglyph described in 1915 by Wisconsin State Archaeologist Charles E. Brown, near the south shore. This find was made by a new group of Illinois enthusiasts inspired enough after reading my book to form The Rock Lake Research Society in 1998. Its founder and president, Archie Eschborn, brought determination, professionalism, and the latest high-tech instruments to bear on the quest. Over the next three years, he and his serious, talented colleagues devoted their energies and intelligence to unraveling its enigma. Another of their fascinating sonar finds included a small village about forty feet beneath the southern middle of the lake on a raised platform surrounded by a standing wall. An apparent roadway led off from the site in a northwesterly direction.

The late March 2000 fly-over that found the Luke and Amos Mounds was the most successful aerial reconnaissance of Rock Lake. A rare combination of variables cooperated to afford extraordinarily clear views down to its bottom. In addition to its crystal clarity after the freshly melted winter ice cap, the surface was unrippled by winds, and sparse cloud cover allowed sufficient sunlight with a minimum of glare off the water. Taking advantage of these all-too-infrequent conditions, Steven Dempsey obtained the best photographs ever taken of the delta formation.

But several new discoveries were also made during that flight, including the Luke and Amos Mounds. As we banked over the southeast quadrant, we were surprised to observe a straight line running out approximately a thousand feet from the shore underwater before disappearing toward the middle of Rock Lake. From our aerial perspective, it might have been a road

"Luke's Mound" in the eastern quadrant of Rock Lake.

or pipeline. Steve's infrared photographs revealed that it ran entirely across the bottom of the lake from east to west. According to the local chamber of commerce, no drainage or pipeline construction ever took place near that area of the lake. Lloyd Hornbostel speculated that the mysterious line might be the terminus of a canal described in the early nineteenth century by Increase Lapham.

The noted archaeological surveyor wrote of a ruined stone feature that extended from the northwest side of Aztalan toward Rock Lake, which he surmised was connected by the waterwork, since plowed over by farmers. During Lloyd's own aerial surveys of the area between the lake and Aztalan in the late 1980s, he detected faint, segmented lines running directly across farmland from the northwestern end of the ceremonial center to the southeastern shore, just where our own fly-over spotted a line going out under the water. Lapham's three-mile-long stone canal may have been discovered.

Michael Cushway, our captain of the late March expeditions, examined the same area between the lake and Aztalan, but found something very different. He noticed that the ground showed every sign of having been under water in the not-too-distant geologic past. Strange, broad, white bands crisscrossed the vicinity, two feet beneath the soil. On close inspection, Michael saw that they were formed of many millions of decomposed marine animals, which could only have been deposited there by a body of water. He believes that at one time in prehistory, Rock Lake must have covered the whole area up to Pipestone Hill, only about a quarter of a mile west of Aztalan. The builders of that ancient city may have actually raised its walls very near the former shoreline of the lake, centuries before it retreated to its present configuration, three miles away. Perhaps that retreat was the flood which engulfed a shallower Rock Lake, drowning the stone monuments gradually being discovered by divers.

His interpretation is the latest and perhaps most credible of the theories used to explain how the structures arrived at the bottom of the lake. Since 1992, geophysicists have learned from orbital Landsat surveys of Wisconsin that the southern part of the state has been sinking at an incredible foot per century. This dramatic fall is generated by isostatic change, in which the land is still on the rebound from the last Ice Age, twelve thousand years ago, as the weight of the retreated glaciers (the size of the Rocky Mountains) moved north. Such a drop would have important consequences for the original Rock Lake, hardly more than a tarn or glacier-carved pool sitting at the bottom of a valley.

As the land progressively fell, the adjacent body of water (what Michael postulates as "Pipestone Lake") emptied itself from the west into the nearby valley, drowning its necropolis of pyramidal mounds, until the lake assumed its present dimensions. The abundance of marine deposits separating Pipestone Hill from Rock Lake at a depth of twenty-four inches beneath present

"Amos Mound" in the eastern quadrant of Rock Lake.

ground level clearly establishes that the three-mile area in between was long ago the bottom of another lake. Laboratory analysis of these deposits may reveal that Pipestone Lake was indeed responsible for the flood that brought the stone sepulchers to the bottom of Rock Lake.

·18·

The Aztec Connection

It was the Mexicans' belief that they had come from the sea, from the region of light (the East) and that their journey's end had finally been at the Atlantic coast.

—*Eduard Seler*

R ock Lake-Aztalan is a wonderful place because it challenges the mind—not with a single intriguing question but with several provocative mysteries that have preoccupied professional and amateur investigators for more than a hundred years.

This latest inquiry has attempted to confront at least some of these enigmas, but many still evade pat solutions. Where, for example, did the people of Rock Lake-Aztalan come from? Why did they choose to settle in southern Wisconsin when they did? Why did they leave? Where did they go? What became of them? Through years of accumulating information compiled by numerous researchers, a picture of what actually happened is beginning to take form. It is a picture far more dramatic and fascinating than anything previously assumed or imagined.

At least the immediate origin of the Aztalaners is among the less controversial questions still connected with the site. They came from what is now southwest Illinois, just across the Mississippi from St. Louis. Today, visitors pass through the modern museum and climb "Monks Mound," all part of an archaeological zone known as Cahokia.

But the public park bears only a faint resemblance to the sprawling metropolis that flourished there a thousand years ago, when thirty thousand people inhabited the greatest ceremonial center north of the Rio Grande. Dozens of pyramidal structures clustered around and beyond a forty-acre plaza at the foot of a gargantuan step-mound fourteen acres square, wider at its base than Egypt's Great Pyramid, over one hundred feet high and made from more than a million cubic feet of soil, completely encased in decorated clay.

Surrounding the city was a twenty-foot-tall stockade of plastered lime, defended by hundreds of watchtowers, more than four miles in circumference, outside of which stood America's version of Stonehenge—Woodhenge. These five precisely arranged circles were composed of identically shaped, red-painted cedar poles oriented to various celestial phenomena.

Cahokia (its real name is unknown) exploded into existence around A.D. 900, growing swiftly to become the dominant cultural and political power of the Mississippi Valley. For two hundred years, the settlement, more populous than contemporary London, prospered and extended its trading networks west to the Rocky Mountains for bear claws, south to the Gulf of Mexico for conch shells, east to the Atlantic seaboard for dinner-plate-size mica flakes and north to the Upper Great Lakes for tons of the highest grade copper in the world. Then, just as abruptly as Cahokia had appeared, it collapsed.[1]

There are some signs of burning having taken place near the northeast corner of the wall, but evidence for major social dislocation is highly equivocal and archaeologists are not sure whether the fire accompanied evacuation or came after it. They know only that, in A.D. 1100, the pre-Columbian

Cahokia at the zenith of its power a thousand years ago.
The colossal Monks Mound towers in the background.

Courtesy Cahokia Museum, Collinsville, Illinois

megalopolis was abandoned en masse, falling into neglect and ruin immediately thereafter.

The date of its sudden demise is our first clue to the origins of Aztalan, which was founded at the same time. In fact, resemblance to Cahokia is so close that no impartial observer can seriously doubt that the Wisconsin site was created, not merely influenced, by the same culture-bearers from southwestern Illinois, three hundred miles away. Even at first glance, Aztalan seems like a scaled-down version of Cahokia. The walls were identically constructed with the same kinds of materials and matched the dimensions of its predecessor. Earthworks, too, included the conical dome, ridge-top, square and step-mounds surmounted by high-gabled temples of wood and prairie grass. The same crops were grown, most of the same trade goods were imported and both sites were located on the banks of major river systems. The tall posts of Woodhenge were astronomical devices repeated in Aztalan, where arrowheads actually manufactured in Cahokia are still being found. Doubtless, they originally belonged to the original Cahokians who arrived at the site that they built up into Aztalan.

Judging from the abundant calendrical information regularly computed through Aztalan, we may presume that the group that left Cahokia to resettle in southern Wisconsin's leading sacred center comprised the astronomers who were formerly in charge at Woodhenge. This supposition is dramatically underscored by the chief astronomical orientation prevailing at both ceremonial centers: Aztalan's Pyramid of the Sun and Cahokia's Monks Mound are aligned to mark sunrise at the winter solstice.

Many ceremonial settlements throughout the Mississippi Valley which sprang into existence after the collapse of Cahokia shared numerous elements in common with each other. But Aztalan alone featured the copious celestial alignments which made it the foremost observatory in pre-Columbian America north of the Rio Grande. Such a unique place could only have been arranged by specialists who carried with them a body of cosmological knowledge and expertise from beyond the Rock River area, and the only conceivable source of native prehistoric astronomy was Cahokia.

Of course, Aztalan, even at its peak population, could never have accounted for the total number of people who left Cahokia. The immigrants did not all head north. Some only journeyed to present-day Carbondale, about eighty miles away, where, at what was later known as the Lynne Site, they duplicated only a fraction of the physical splendor of their former capital. Many more sailed the Ohio River into southern Indiana, where, in place of today's Evansville, they raised Angel Mounds, a city very much like Aztalan. Others cruised up the Wabash to found similar settlements outside Vincennes. Still others went down the Mississippi to create pyramids and ceremonial enclosures in what is now Missouri and Kentucky, such as the Towasahgy and Wickliffe Mounds.

Garcilosso de la Vega, the chronicler who traveled with De Soto's expedition through the South in the sixteenth century, described an Aztalan-like fortress in Georgia's Harlin County, near Savannah.[2] Still other sites of similar or identical descriptions occurred to the east, around Lake Erie, beyond into Virginia and the Carolinas, even Connecticut, near New London.[3] They represented the scattered population formerly concentrated in Cahokia.

We may surmise that each of the walled towns was settled by a particular tribe or leading family from that greater ceremonial center following its collapse. Aztalan was part of this mass migration from Cahokia that spread south, north and east out of the Mississippi Valley in the early twelfth century. Of them all, Aztalan was the most complex and important, if not the most populous.

The identification of the inhabitants of Aztalan with the ancient civilizers of Cahokia still does not tell us who they were, however. Where did they come from before they suddenly arrived in southern Illinois?

In attempting an answer to this potentially volatile question, we should begin with the name itself. Standard references contend that "Aztalan" is a misnomer, that the real name of the fortified settlement on the west bank of the Crawfish River is lost to history. Its ruins were discovered in October 1835 and were known among pioneers as the "Ancient City," a resident Ho Chunk reference to the site.[4] The following January, it was surveyed for the first time by Nathaniel F. Hyer, a well-read judge and early settler in the area. Supposedly, he presumed that the ancient city was the legendary home of the Aztecs, who claimed to have arrived in the Valley of Mexico from somewhere in the north. Hyer thus erroneously dubbed the place "Aztalan," as the Aztecs' ancestral homeland. The name persists to the present day, although archaeologists have long dismissed any conceivable connection between prehistoric Wisconsin and events south of the Rio Grande. Lynne Goldstein's conviction that "there is nothing about Aztalan which is similar to Aztec civilization" was academic dogma for most of the twentieth century.[5]

Despite well-entrenched scholastic opinion, many disturbing features about Aztalan do indeed point clearly toward Mesoamerica, and far more interestingly, reveal a great deal about the Rock Lake story and its people— their fate and the reason for their occupation of Wisconsin. In publishing these highly controversial concepts for the first time, I am aware that their evidence is not universally acknowledged by everyone who has shared in our Rock Lake researches, let alone most professionals, who scoff at the very notion of any parallels between Aztalan and the Aztec world. Prehistorians have tended to sharply divide pre-Columbian civilizations into Andean, Middle American and North American cultural arenas, discounting any significant physical contact among them. Ideas may have been gradually and unintentionally transmitted during chance encounters, nothing more. But such a rigid compartmentalization of the past has already been dealt some serious blows.

It is now known, for example, that the ancient Mexicans had a system of actual hard currency called "axe-monies," which originated with Ecuadoran merchantmen, who spread the same concept to Peru and Chile. In Moundville, Ohio, the grave of an important personage was recently opened to reveal a necklace made of parakeet bills,[6] and ceremonial pipes found in Tennessee were crafted of stone from South American quarries.[7] Important material evidence does indeed exist to demonstrate that the Americas were not so isolated and disconnected as most scholars insist. Nor did the inhabitants of Aztalan live in a complete vacuum, oblivious to the rest of the outside world. Far from it. We have already seen that their trading networks stretched to the Atlantic seaboard and the Gulf of Mexico.

Wisconsin's first clue to some connection with the Valley of Mexico is the very name, "Aztalan." Increase Lapham, a skilled, early surveyor of ancient earthworks in the Upper Midwest, assumed that the site was so described by

Judge Hyer after he had read Alexander von Humbolt's account of Aztec legends that identified "Aztlan" as their ancestral homeland.[8] Hyer was well versed in von Humbolt's studies, so it is improbable that he would have consistently misspelled so important a name. Moreover, the Aztecs identified Aztlan as a volcanic island in the east, "the sunrise sea"; i.e., the Atlantic Ocean. It was from here, they said, that their ancestors first arrived in Vera Cruz, on the eastern shore of Mexico. In the many generations since then, they wandered to a place called "the Lake of the Seven Caves," or "the Womb"—Chicomoztoc. Located in the far north, it was their place of residence just prior to their final resettlement in the Valley of Mexico.[9] Since Hyer knew all this, one presumes he would have more sensibly referred to the Wisconsin enclosure as Chicomoztoc, instead of a misspelling of "Aztlan."

His own account of the site, the first published description of Aztalan, and released in an 1837 edition of New York's *Greenwich Eagle,* leaves no doubt that "Aztalan" was not invented by the judge, but was, after all, a title used by the resident Ho Chunk to describe the mound group long before the arrival of European pioneers in the early nineteenth century. The name is gibberish in any language spoken by Great Lakes tribes and in any Native American tongue north of the Rio Grande. The Ho Chunk preserved "Aztalan" in oral tradition without understanding its meaning, other than as an old reference to the walled town. Remarkably, it translates perfectly into the language spoken by the Aztecs. In Nahuatl, a literal translation of the word is "Place-near-Water," a syllabic transformative of $A(z)tl$ = water, a = near, lan = place. More usefully translated, it means "Water Town." Remarkably, ten miles northwest of Aztalan and connected to it by the Crawfish River is modern Watertown. This name, too, is a survivor from pioneer days, when resident Indians were still willing to speak of the ancient "foreign chiefs" who occupied the area.

It is apparent, then, that Judge Hyer did not merely assign the name "Aztalan" to the Wisconsin mound group because of some vague suspicion that the site was perhaps a legendary homeland. Rather, it was remembered by the local Ho Chunk as a prehistoric reference undoubtedly used by the vanished builders of the fortified village. The ancient authenticity of the name was reaffirmed by an early, respected collector of Native American lore in regional Wisconsin, S. D. Peet, whose research revealed that "The name Aztalan was derived from a tradition, which was said to be common among the Indians, to the effect that a people who were partially civilized, and who possessed tools and implements of all kinds, who cultivated the soil and built houses, had, at a previous time, come from the northeast and settled in this State, and here built a city, but having become dissatisfied, after the lapse of a hundred years, burned their city, and proceeded south to Mexico, which they conquered, and have ever since retained."[10]

While the Aztalaners certainly came from Cahokia, in the *southwest*, their alleged northeasterly origins mentioned here are more probably a partial recollection of the busy copper mining routes that were so extensively traveled from Aztalan to Michigan's Upper Peninsula. They were doubtless the same people who immigrated en masse from Cahokia to Wisconsin and to downstate Indiana's Angel Mounds around A.D. 1100. So, too, abundant carbon-dated remains from Aztalan confirm that the site was occupied for two hundred years, not merely a single century. Conceptions of time are mostly blurred in oral accounts and "many years ago" may refer to incidents millennia in the past or only a few generations back.

A significant piece of evidence underscoring "Aztalan's" verity is an archaeological zone some three hundred miles to the southeast on the banks of the Wabash River, in Merom, Indiana. Little known to most researchers, it was a fortified town that flourished from the early twelfth century. A wall ran almost a mile to enclose at least forty-five gypsum-covered houses, five dome-shaped, square and ridge-top mounds, together with a trio of fresh-water springs. A thirty-foot-thick wall or ramp made of mixed clay and limestone abutted the south end of the ramparts. Around A.D. 1320, the settlement was inexplicably abandoned.

If all this sounds remarkably similar to events in southern Wisconsin, the parallel draws surprisingly closer when we learn that the prehistoric Indiana town is called—Aztalan. Like the far away Ho Chunk, resident Potawatomis and Delawares preserved this name associated with the Wabash site, although they did not understand its meaning except that it had been used long ago by the unknown builders and inhabitants.[11]

Apparently, "Aztalan" was their generic term for a river town and was applied to affiliated sites throughout the Mississippi Valley. It was preserved in the folk traditions of Plains Indians, who, for good or ill, had dealings with these mysterious culture-bearers. An oral tradition has passed the name down to the present day. Even among archaeologists, the Early Post Classic Period in ancient Mexico at the start of the Aztec epoch (circa A.D. 1100) is referred to as "the Aztalan Complex." If they decry any conceivable connection between Mesoamerica and prehistoric Wisconsin, why have they chosen the name "Aztalan" to identify the beginning of the Aztec World? As for the real name of what is presently known as Aztalan, which was merely a descriptive term for a river town, or "watertown," there is more than a little evidence to suggest that it may indeed have been the "Womb" of the Aztecs, the Seven Caves of Chicomoztoc, through the site's intrinsic relation with Rock Lake. After all, "Aztalan's" identification as a Nahuatl word is a powerful link with Mesoamerica.

But what did the Aztecs themselves say about their immediate origins in the north? They affirmed that sometime after their arrival from the island of Aztlan, they migrated to a lake in the far north, where they established their first American kingdom. They never referred to themselves as "Aztecs," a title coined by their Spanish conquerors because of the natives' professed oceanic origins. They actually comprised seven families known collectively as the Nahuatlacs, which means something like "the Old Sacred Ones from the Sea," a plain allusion to Aztlan.

As a collective tribe they called themselves the Meztl, or the People of Meztliapan, the "Lake of the Moon," the same description assigned to Rock Lake by the Native American elder who passed this tribal tradition on to Dr. Scherz.[12] There is, too, a general physical resemblance between Texcoco, located in the Aztec Mexican capital, and Rock Lake itself. They are roughly shaped like a figure eight, with the larger body of water to the south connected to the smaller in the north, perhaps because both were artificially created.

The Meztl's new home was Chicomoztoc, the Lake of the Seven Caves, a metaphor for "womb," implying their septenary tribal origins. As Morgan wrote, "This tradition embodies one significant fact of a kind that could not have been invented; namely, that the seven tribes were of immediate common origin, the fact being confirmed by their dialects; and a second fact of importance, that they came from the north. It shows that they were originally one people, who had fallen into seven and more tribes by the natural process of segmentation."[13]

Mexico's leading expert on the Aztecs underscores the veracity of northerly beginnings: "Perhaps this explains why the traditions dealing with the migrations of so many tribes of Mesoamerica say that these tribes came from Chicomoztoc; that is, from the Womb."[14]

The Aztec symbol for the womb (and hence, Chicomoztoc) was the spiral, the same symbol that appears most commonly on pottery found in Aztalan, where the design was the sacred emblem there and related to the movements of recurring astronomical phenomena. "Chicomoztoc" was also related to the Nahuatl word for copper, *toc chichimec,* or "red woman." Considering the vital role that Rock Lake-Aztalan played in the ancient copper mining, the name of the Aztec northerly origins take on a mutually validating symbolism.

Surviving Aztec paintings of Chicomoztoc depict it as a small lake dotted with tiny islands and bordered by forests, which is just how Rock Lake appeared when Aztalan was flourishing in the thirteenth century. Remarkably, some of the chiefs portrayed in the Chicomoztoc representation are bearded, with decidedly non-Native-American facial features. Until their mixture with Spanish invaders, the native Mexicans were beardless, except, interestingly enough, for their emperor, Moctezuma III, and the adult males of his royal family.

Ho Chunk Indians told nineteenth-century researchers that the ancient inhabitants of Aztalan abandoned their settlement and migrated south, just as the Aztecs claimed their immediate forefathers traveled into the Valley of Mexico from the north. These complimentary traditions are reinforced by the founding of the Aztec capital in 1325, which is precisely the same time period in which Aztalan was evacuated. Alfredo Caso writes that, in the creation of Tenochtitlan, the Aztecs wanted "to establish themselves on another island also located in the middle of the lake, which would have not only the same physical but also the same mythical conditions as the place from which they had come."[15] The place they chose was called Texcoco, another "Lake of the Moon."

The Aztec foundation story told that a "stone cactus" stood on an island in the middle of Lake Texcoco. With the building of Tenochtitlan, it was enshrined in a conical temple structure at the precise center of the new capital. "Tenochtitlan" means literally "Place of *(lan)* the Stone *(tetl)* Cactus *(nochtli)*." This "stone cactus" was nothing more than an esoteric metaphor for a solar-aligned monolith of the kind discovered on the islets of Rock Lake, an identification made all the more certain when we learn that it was upon this "stone cactus" that an eagle perched, an event that told the Aztecs to remain in the Valley of Mexico and build their city.

The eagle was their symbol of the sun, so its appearance in relation to the "stone cactus," a monolithic sundial, means that the Aztec astronomers calculated the correct solar time and place for settlement. In fact, they referred to the Valley of Mexico as the Land of the Sun, Huitztlampa. We remember the conical mounds of Aztalan's Greenwood Group, whose alignment posts cast shadows from the sun to mark significant positions in the solar calendar. At Angel Mounds, Aztalan's sister-city in southern Indiana, conical projections atop the large temple-mound were associated with the rising sun.[16]

The Aztec construction of Tenochtitlan recalls the irrigation feats of the inhabitants of Aztalan. As Lewis H. Morgan wrote, "Having the sagacity to perceive the advantages of the location, they succeeded by means of causeways and dikes in surrounding their pueblo with an artificial pond of large extent. The level of Lake Texcoco being higher then than at present, it gave them, when the whole work was completed, the most secure position of any tribe in the valley. The mechanical engineering by which they accomplished this result was one of the greatest achievements of the Aztecs, and one without which they would not probably have risen above the level of the surrounding tribes. Independence and prosperity followed, and in time a controlling interest over the valley tribes."[17]

The ancient engineers of Aztalan similarly employed causeways and, according to Native American tradition, could raise and lower water levels at Rock Lake, possibly going so far as to inundate Tyranena with a sluice canal from a tributary of the Rock River. We recall their stone aqueduct that some investigators believe may have connected Aztalan with Rock Lake, three miles away. So too, the fifteenth-century Aztec emperor, Nazahualcoyot ("Hungry Coyote"), constructed a colossal aqueduct nearly ten miles long to irrigate the territories around Lake Texcoco.[18] Clearly, the construction of massive irrigation projects was shared by both Aztecs and the people of Aztalan.

The walls of private dwellings in Tenochtitlan and of the houses behind Aztalan's enclosure were coated with white limestone and gypsum plaster. Even domestic building styles were identical. Furthermore, while the Aztecs built pyramids of stone, their Olmec predecessors constructed pyramidal earthworks encased in variously colored clay, the identical technique used by the mound builders throughout the Mississippi valley, including Cahokia and Aztalan.

Some of the more obvious physical comparisons between the Aztalan and Aztec cultures include the temple buildings both constructed. Wisconsin's Pyramid of the Sun, a step pyramid, was surmounted by a steeply gabled shrine, its walls made of wattle and daub with a dried-grass roof; the same kind of shrine adorned the summits of the Aztec step-pyramids in Tenochtitlan. Among archaeological digs at many Mississippian sites, strange, beautifully crafted baton-like ceremonial objects, usually made from semiprecious stone, have been recovered. The Maya equivalent of a major domo in the service of his chief was similarly entrusted with a stone baton as the symbol of his authority.

Head elongation, in which the skulls of newborn infants were made to grow in an oblong shape by placing them between a pair of boards, was practiced by both Aztecs and the people of Aztalan. The deformed heads were considered particularly aesthetic and may have been associated with the upper classes. This peculiar attention to the human head in life carried over into cult practices after death. We remember the respectful interment of a headless "giant" outside the walls of Aztalan, the seventy-nine-foot-long headless man earthwork just beyond and the effigy of a decapitated anthropomorphic figure under Rock Lake.

One of the most important Aztec ceremonies took place every April 5, when a man selected for his tall stature and handsome appearance was costumed to impersonate the sun god, Texcatlipocha, in a ritual drama that climaxed with his beheading. As Hultkranz writes, "It was in his role as the sun-god completing the yearly cycle that Texcatlipocha was this incarnation of a man. In the fifth month, the sun passed through the zenith for the first time since the winter solstice and then the old Texcatlipocha died in the form of a captured warrior. In this way, the sun-god set out on his New Year cycle and the rainy season began."[19]

The relationship between this Aztec ritual and the headless mounds and burial at Rock Lake-Aztalan is inescapable, particularly the calendrical aspects of Texcatlipocha's solar ceremony, which reflects ancient Wisconsin's alignment posts oriented to various positions of the sun. Aztalan's skeleton without a skull most likely belonged to the central player in one of these religious dramas.

Ritual beheading preceded the Aztec domination of Mexico by many generations. The "Codex-style" funerary vase from southern Campeche, now at Princeton University in New Jersey, painted in the eighth century by the classic Mayas, depicts a man being decapitated. The figure portrays 7-Hunahpu. He and his twin brother, 1-Hunahpu, were symbolically executed to represent an astral myth, wherein the planet Venus appears to die and resurrect itself in its aspects as the evening and morning star.[20]

We recall Aztalan's Pyramid of Venus with its ten entombed bodies oriented to the rising of Venus. In other words, the decapitation-cult originated in ancient Mesoamerica, whence it was imported into Illinois and Wisconsin by the late classic Maya, who resettled at Cahokia around the turn of the tenth century. Moreover, the severed head appears to have been invariable associated with heavenly objects: the sun (Huitzlipocha), Venus (Hunahpu) or the moon (Coyolxauqui, as portrayed by the famous crystal skull), again underscoring the complex astronomy shared from Aztalan and Cahokia to Tenochtitlan of the Aztecs and Chichen Itza of the Mayas.

The headless-man cult undoubtedly preceded Aztalan-Aztec practice, because the Mayas were acquainted with the same bizarre ritual. As Moreley wrote, "After death, the head was severed from the body and cooked in order to remove all flesh. It was then sawed in half from side to side, care being taken to preserve the jaw, nose, eyes and forehead in one piece. Upon this as a form the features of the dead man were filled in with a kind of gum. Such

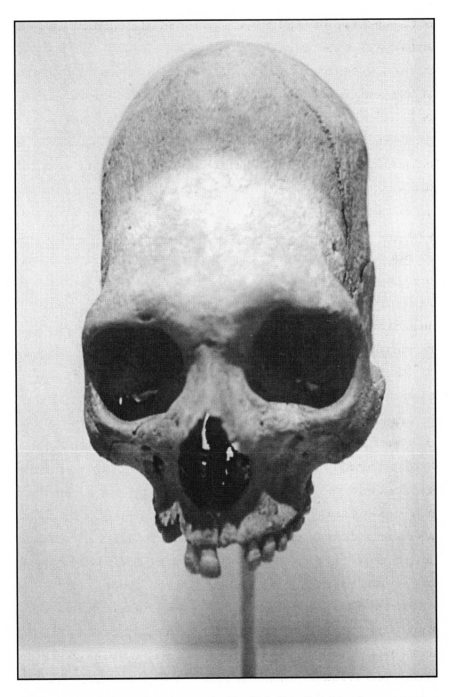

Head elongation was practiced by the ruling elite of Aztalan.

was their extraordinary skill in this particular work that the finished mask is said to have appeared exactly like the countenance in life. The carefully prepared faces, together with the statues containing the ashes of the dead, were deposited with their idols. Every feast day, meats were set before them so they should lack for nothing in that other world whither they had gone."[21]

Thus we are assured not only of the ancient origins of the headless-man cult, but that Aztalan's decapitated "giant" was memorialized in the same kind of pre-Columbian forensic reconstruction achieved in Yucatan before A.D. 900. Should his head ever be discovered in good condition, we would once more look upon the face of a native of Aztalan. This explanation for so otherwise inexplicable a burial is a significant link connecting prehistoric Wisconsin with its Mesoamerican origins.

Another compelling cultural common denominator linking prehistoric Wisconsin with Mesoamerica was found among the stone monuments at the bottom of Rock Lake, when scuba divers retrieved several deer bones (all leg bones) from various pyramidal structures. Investigators theorized they may be the remains of a funeral feast and/or sacrifice for the honored dead entombed in the necropolis. Whistles fashioned from the leg bones of deer were used by the ancient Mexicans to accompany religious rituals on behalf of Huitzlipochtli, the legendary sun god who led the Aztecs' ancestors into the Valley of Mexico. He was portrayed at their capital, Tenochtitlan, wearing a deer skull on his forehead. Meanwhile, in the Ohio Valley, several pre-Columbian graves belonging to shamans have yielded crowns of deer antlers made to fit over the forehead, the identical arrangement worn by Huitzlipochtli.

Ake Hultkranz writes, "It is noteworthy that deer were extinct in the Valley of Mexico long before the appearance of the Aztecs there. They had disappeared in the early classical period."[22] In other words, the Aztecs brought deer symbolism with them from some place where the animal was still abundant; i.e., from the north. The creature was so ritually important to the Aztecs

Native artist's rendition (Codex Mendoza, circa 1550) representing the northerly origins of the Aztecs from Chicomoztoc (Rock Lake). The eagle (Huitzlipochtli, the sun god) fights with a snake (a water sign), symbolizing the drought which immediately preceded the evacuation of Aztalan. The animals are struggling on an islet above a "stone cactus," or rock pyramid, used as a sundial. The resemblance of this illustration to Rock Lake even includes the animal effigy mounds discovered by sonar and (to right of cactus) the bulrushes that grew out of the water centuries ago. The islet itself is another sunken feature detected during a 1999 fly-over.

that they named one of the day-signs of their calendar after it: Mazatl. Clearly, the deer was venerated by both the inhabitants of Rock Lake and the Aztecs in at least a similar fashion, yet another indication of the fascinating relationship between these two peoples.

When divers found a bone inside one of the sunken structures in 1990, they were excited at the prospect of its human identity. But their enthusiasm turned to disappointment when they were told it belonged to a deer, not to some ancient pyramid dweller. They need not have been so discouraged, however. For all the innumerable dives that have taken place there, only five bones have ever been found in Rock Lake, all of them belonging to deer, of great age and recovered from the stone pyramids.

Mike Kutska's Narcosis Knights made a particularly revealing discovery in 1968, when the bone they found was among a cache of broken clamshells resembling the debris of a feast and deposited inside the wall of one of the structures. It seems difficult to imagine deer straying out onto the lake in winter, dying on the ice cap and sinking only on top of sunken pyramids. No less ludicrous is the notion of boaters munching on venison and tossing the bones into the water, where they fortuitously sank onto the stone structures.

In any case, all the deer bones are centuries old, although precise dating is not possible. Moreover, all except one, which was too small to break, had been cracked open; the ancient inhabitants of Aztalan were notorious for their love of marrow, which they extracted from broken bones. Numerous identically broken deer bones have, in fact, been excavated throughout Aztalan. The bone retrieved from Rock Lake by Jason Bucholtz shows several long scratches that could have been made by a blade used to trim off the meat and fat. The deer bones fit perfectly into our interpretation of the lake bottom as a City of the Dead, at which funeral feasts, common to many cultures around the world, were held when the deceased was interred within the stone monument. The bones recovered by divers are probably the remains of those ritual meals.

The most popular deity of the Aztecs was Quetzalcoatl, the Feathered Serpent, the man-god who brought enlightenment to Middle America, where he was synonymous with the planet Venus. Representations of him in sacred art show Quetzalcoatl wearing the *ocelocopili,* a high, conical helmet made of ocelot skin. So too, a stone pipe fashioned in the image of a man wearing the ocelocopili, now at Madison's Historical Museum, was found in Aztalan. It was there that the positions of Venus were observed and the ten people buried in the Pyramid of Venus were aligned on a north-

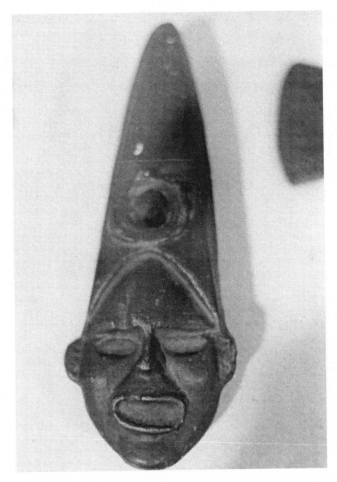

Stone pipe from Aztalan Wisconsin Historical Museum, Madison

west-southeast axis, an orientation associated throughout Mesoamerica with the rising of Quetzalcoatl's planet.

His ocelocopili connects the Aztecs with far more than Aztalan, however. In the Old World story of Cadmus, the Greek myth with so many startling parallels to Rock Lake, the hero was traditionally depicted wearing a "Phoenician cap," a tall, conical helmet worn not only by Phoenicians, but popular with seafarers along the Aegean coasts of Asia Minor, to Troy, and identical to the headgear sported by Quetzalcoatl.

.19.

Axe-Money

A man rose out of the sea, a hero from the waves. His helmet was of copper, copper the boots on his feet, copper the gauntlets on his hands, copper their lacings, copper the belt at his body, copper the axe in his belt.

—From the Finnish Munapojka,

The Boy Born in the Egg

The Ecuadoran Canari are vital to understanding the connection between Aztalan and the Aztec world. They represent a key to unlock perhaps the final mystery of Rock Lake, its sunken buildings and the destiny of its people.

Let us insert that key into the turn of the tenth century A.D. It was a time of large-scale inexplicable transformation throughout North America. The Mayas suddenly evacuated all their colossal ceremonial centers across Yucatan, abandoned en masse the rich and complex civilization they had labored to create for more than a thousand years.

At the same moment, the "Mound Builders" entered the Mississippi Valley, raising impressive walled sacred centers and pyramids aligned with celestial phenomena. Simultaneous with this cultural shift to a northern focus, the copper mines of Michigan's Upper Peninsula, which had lain dormant for more than two millennia, were abruptly reopened and intensively worked. Once again, tons of raw copper were extracted and shipped away. Some of it reached the Mississippian capital, the megalopolis at Cahokia, Illinois, where vast, rolled sheets of hammered copper were part of the rich grave goods of a powerful personage discovered during excavation of a large pyramidal burial mound.

The copper went to other ceremonial sites—Spiro, in Oklahoma; Etowah, in Georgia; Indiana's Angel Mounds, and elsewhere. But their importation accounted for only a fraction of the total amount mined. Where did the bulk of the copper go? Why did the Mississippians mine it in such huge quantities, if not for their own use? The copper miners who preceded them in the second millennium B.C. apparently shipped their cargoes overseas to make possible the Old World Bronze Age. But regular transatlantic contacts or markets did not exist with Medieval Europe. These questions seem too mysterious for solutions. Or are they? Their answers appear to be found among the Canari of Ecuador.

Simultaneous with the relocation of the Mayas from Yucatan to the Mississippi Valley and their reopening of Michigan's copper mines, the numerically insignificant Canari rose to sudden influence and affluence as sea traders all along the western coasts of Middle and South America. By far their most important contribution to pre-Columbian civilization was the introduction into Mexico and Peru of axe-monies, or, more properly stated, the concept of axe-monies. These were small, non-utilitarian copper axes used as actual currency to purchase goods and accumulate wealth, functioning the same as coins in Western societies.

The Canari introduced the know-how to work these axe-monies. Some were made of bronze in combinations of arsenic and/or tin, much the same process developed by Bronze Age Europeans. It seems the Canari knew the technique of producing arsenical copper, or "arsenic bronze," for many generations, perhaps from deeply ancient transatlantic contacts. But only after the Maya evacuation of Yucatan did they share their knowledge with others, and Mexican metallurgy did indeed begin with the Canari arrival in Oaxaca, around A.D. 900.

The axe-monies rapidly became the basis of Mesoamerican economy, recognized as legitimate tribute and acceptable as ritual offerings as well as a means of exchange. They were even minted, after a fashion, and standardized into specific sizes: 7.7 to 8.9 cm, 6.5 to 6.9 cm and 1.2 to 4.5 cm. They were mass produced "often in great quantity."[1] More than thirteen thousand *hachuelas,* as the Spaniards called them, were found in only one vessel at a Canari grave in Itda, Ecuador. Hosler writes that "finds of hundreds, at times thousands, are typical in the central Milagro-Quevedo/Manteno culture area. Axe-monies constitute one of the most abundant metal artifact types in Mesoamerica."[2]

A spectacular discovery of axe-monies was made near Oaxaca, where a terra-cotta pot contained twenty-three dozen cloth-bound and neatly stacked hachuelas, a king's ransom. A mass burial of seventeen individuals similar to Cahokia's pyramidal grave at Huaca Meno (Baton Grande) included cinnabar, spondylus shells (both elements also found at the Illinois site), lapis lazuli (shades of Ancient Egypt!) and five hundred kilograms of copper. Copper-made tribute collected from Michoacan by the conquistadors and stored at the Casa de Municion in Mexico City amounted to five hundred shields and thirteen chests of axe-monies. Lima's Anthropological Museum has a cask with a volume of three cubic meters filled to the brim with copper currency.

But the Canari who trafficked in mineral wealth were even richer. One of their tombs near the important Inca fortress of Ingapirka yielded enough axe-monies to equal the annual tribute of a major *en camienda*. Another Canari grave site at Gupan contained three thousand hachuelas, or 333 pounds of copper currency.

The source for this vast copper supply existed in neither South nor Middle America, but was mined in Michigan's Upper Peninsula. All investigators agree that the vast majority of copper used by Mesoamerican and Andean civilizations prior to the early fourteenth century came from the Upper Great Lakes region.[3] The Michigan connection with axe-money trade and manufacture was positively established when Bruce Johanson, the historian of Ontonagon, found "a strange, thin copper axe in one of the old mines that looks almost like a stage weapon"—a hachuela of the kind shipped by the Canari and used in the markets of Mexico and Peru.[4]

Now the importance of Cahokia and its own great wealth are explained by the copper its miners extracted and transported to Middle America, where copper was the basis of Mesoamerica's economic existence. The hachuelas came into being at the same time Cahokia set up in Illinois, where it sat at the crossroads of copper production from the north and shipment to the south. When Cahokia was abandoned two centuries later, its leaders established themselves anew in Rock Lake-Aztalan, which had been undoubtedly known to them for many generations before as a place of sacred pilgrimage for its ancient necropolis and as a stopover outpost from the Michigan mines. Now it was Aztalan's turn to become rich, as the copper trade continued unabated. We recall the long building behind Aztalan's enclosure, in which large supplies of raw copper were temporarily stored.

But around 1320, the bottom fell out of prehistoric Wisconsin's prosperity, when natural copper deposits were discovered in northern Mexico. Mesoamerican societies no longer needed to trade for copper from distant Aztalan. Even Canari-manufacture of axe-monies abruptly ceased with the opening of the Mexican mines.

Dorothy Hosler has shown that Mexican copper metallurgy began before the tenth century and completed its first phase about four hundred years later, when local binary copper-silver alloys, copper-arsenic and copper-tin bronzes replaced the silver-flecked copper imported at greater expense from the Upper Great Lakes.[5] This second phase, which clearly begins after A.D. 1300 and continued until the Spanish conquest, occurred at the same moment Aztalan was suddenly evacuated. It doubtless explains why the mining center was abandoned forever. With the discovery of an abundant resident copper source, Michigan supplies were no longer needed.

Appropriately, the Upper Peninsula mines were swiftly vacated after the beginning of the fourteenth century, just as they had been 2,500 years before, their tools remaining in place to this day as though the miners might return to their work at any moment.

But they never came back, and many modern researchers have speculated that their withdrawal from Rock Lake-Aztalan was caused by an extended drought that ravaged America's Middle West. Even Ho Chunk traditions speak of a long, dry period, during which the inhabitants of Aztalan deserted their city. The Aztecs, who we are identifying with the post-Cahokian immigrants to Wisconsin, practiced human sacrifice during periods of drought, rituals they may have brought with them from the north, where severe conditions prompted them to such bloody acts of propitiation. Even the Aztec myth and emblem of an eagle (the sun) fighting a snake (water) has been interpreted as a representation of drought.[6]

Underscoring this cultural evidence is the fact that rainfall from America's Southwest to the Upper Great Lakes region occurs in 550-year cycles of drought, and that the pattern reached its optimum just after A.D. 1100. This was the same date Aztalan was founded, followed two hundred years later by the onset of a six-year drought and the simultaneous abandonment of the Rock Lake area. The early fourteenth century is, after all, known as the Little

Ice Age, in which temperatures dropped radically from Greenland across the Northern Hemisphere, ushering in cold, dry air.[7]

While a drought may have contributed to their evacuation of southern Wisconsin, it does not seem plausible that difficult weather alone was responsible for the decision of the inhabitants of Aztalan to leave. They had certainly experienced extreme natural conditions before—tornadoes, ruinous hot summers, prairie fires, bad winters—so it seems unlikely that even a prolonged drought would force them to give up their lucrative location as middlemen for the pre-Columbian economies of Meso- and South America.

Discovery of the Mexican copper mines after A.D. 1300 was more probably the real reason for vacating Aztalan. The Wisconsin clearing-house was simply no longer required. Its sudden fall, the shift to a second phase in Middle American metallurgy and the opening of the new mines all took place simultaneously. The bad news from Mexico coincided with a severe drought, which the Aztalaners interpreted as a clear sign from the gods that their luck had turned against them.

But the real story may not have been quite so simple, either. The economic shift away from Wisconsin and the accompanying bad weather were unquestionably primary and abetting causes. But some internal social dilemma may have also contributed to the abandonment of Aztalan. While very similar in numerous physical details to other Mississippian ceremonial centers, the Wisconsin site is distinct from all the rest because of the cannibalism that took place behind its walls during its final years and because of the manner of its destruction. Some researchers believe that elements of Aztalan's ruling hierarchy may have intermarried with the resident Plains Indians, who were themselves cannibals. Even in historic times, several Wisconsin tribes engaged in cannibalism.

The "outsiders" now allowed into the sacred precinct as part of the controlling aristocracy brought with them different religious customs, which included ritual consumption of human flesh. These abhorrent practices sparked a schism that divided Aztalan society between new followers of the introduced death-cult of the natives and traditional adherents of the old religion from Cahokia with its emphasis on the recurring movements of the heavenly bodies.

The social break came to a head with the permanent suspension of all trade from Middle America and the simultaneous drought that settled over the area. Both events were seen (or, perhaps, used) by the original culture-bearers as curses called down upon them by the gods offended by a sacrilegious cannibalism permitted to flourish within the ceremonial precinct. Aztalan had been built and employed as a sacred center, but such abominable behavior was the worst blasphemy against its holiness.

Fire is an archetypal method of purgation recognized by peoples around the world from prehistoric to modern times, and the walls of Aztalan were certainly burned. The conflagration was total, consuming every square foot within the twenty-one-acre complex. Even the worst battles, especially in fourteenth-century North America, were rarely if ever so complete in their devastation. Rather, the charred evidence of Aztalan's last day argues persuasively that the ceremonial site was deliberately, methodically torched by its own inhabitants.

Here, too, Ho Chunk tribal accounts report that the residents burned their city, then migrated southward. We may assume that the traditional inhabitants of Aztalan gained the upper hand and purified their desecrated sacred center with a consuming fire. Of all the related Mississippian citadels, Aztalan alone ended in so total a blaze. The towering flames rising from its two miles of ramparts raged through the night, an awe-inspiring holocaust that burned its image indelibly into the tribal memory of the Plains Indians left behind.

·20·

The Lord of Time

He who dwells in the clouds, the Old God, he who inhabits the
shadows of the land of the dead, the Lord of Fire and of Time.
—From the Aztec Annals of Cuauhtitlan

While the purifying intentions of its inhabitants explain the destruction of Aztalan, why did they forsake the entire area and migrate in a body as far south as the Valley of Mexico?

Given their proficiency as mariners, the evacuation was most likely carried out in vessels traveling the inland waterways from the Crawfish to the Rock River, down the Mississippi into the Gulf of Mexico. We have already seen that their actions around A.D. 1320 were prompted by economic necessity and possibly socio-religious dislocation. Now a third likely cause must be added to the complex story of a people in crisis.

Had the copper trade not failed and the cult schism never occurred, the people of Aztalan would have still vacated their sacred center when they did, although they would not have torched it. Across the Mississippi valley and throughout the South, all the related settlements were deserted at the same time. Aztalan's sister-city on the Ohio River, Indiana's Angel Mounds, saw the departure of its culture-bearers in the early fourteenth century, as did Etowah in Georgia, Spiro Mounds in Oklahoma and so on. In these other fortified towns, the inhabitants suddenly picked up their belongings and vanished.

When the inhabitants of Aztalan set fire to and then abandoned their ceremonial city, not all of them migrated south into the Valley of Mexico, however. Recollections of that mass movement are still preserved in the oral traditions of several Plains Indian tribes. At least one broke away on its own to become a splinter group, settling finally in the Rio Grande valley of what is now New Mexico. These were the Tewa, the Pueblo Indians, who still venerate a tribal memory of their long trek from Rock Lake:

"Yonder in the north there is singing on the lake. There we take our being. Yonder in the north rain stands over the land. Yonder in the north stands forth at twilight the arc of a rainbow. There we have our being."[1]

Mention of "singing on the lake," rain and the rainbow allude to ceremonies at Rock Lake to dispel the drought, which played so important a role in the fate of Aztalan. The Tewa say their ancestors originated from under Sandy Place Lake in the north.[2] "Sandy Beach" has been a local reference to Rock Lake for time out of mind, and today specifically defines the south end of the lake. That the Tewa envision their forefathers emerging out of this body of water is at once reminiscent of the sunken burial monuments and the "womb" of Lake Chicomoztoc, which the Aztecs claimed was their ancestral place of origin.

The Tewa's primeval mother goddesses, while dwelling in Sandy Place Lake, were called "Blue Corn Woman Near to Summer" and "White Corn Woman Near to Ice," which mythically describes Rock Lake's location in southern Wisconsin, just below the hard snowfall line, where summers are mild but winter is closer than in New Mexico.[3] The Tewa built kivas, ceremonial centers commemorating their beginnings in Sandy Place Lake, and "earth navels."

They made round houses open to the southeast, the same orientation found in the spherical homes of Aztalan and associated with the Mesoamerican veneration of Quetzalcoatl's planet, Venus. These residential dwellings were also part of the "mother earth navel," recalling the Aztec Seven Wombs of Lake Chicomoztoc. The Tewa erected sacred buildings that resembled colossal anthills, the same donut-shaped, vision-quest burial mounds found atop Dunn County's high cemetery and today encountered by scuba divers in Rock Lake. Clearly, the Tewa were part of a migration from "Sandy Place," or Rock Lake, that involved simultaneous evacuation from other ceremonial centers throughout the Mississippi valley and beyond.

But how much bearing the Little Ice Age, with its prolonged drought, may have had on these evacuations from the Midwest is doubtful. Certainly, the collapse of the copper trade did not affect all the Mississippian citadels.

What, then, was responsible for all the loosely connected ceremonial centers scattered from Wisconsin to Georgia winding down at the same time? The answer is simple and comprehensively correct: a calendar. One of the major elements in common among the various walled ceremonial centers was their concurrent function as astronomical observatories.

To be sure, Cahokia in Illinois and Aztalan in Wisconsin were extraordinary for their abundant celestial alignments, but any of the centers could at least compute major solar positions. And although the ancient astronomers left behind no written records, we may reasonably surmise from the great diversity of their stellar, lunar and solar orientations that above all they worshiped time. They may have felt oppressed by it, or perhaps they strove to live in harmony with its cycles. In either case, their obvious attention to the movements of the heavens clearly defines an obsession with the regular passage of cycles in nature. Here, too, the mound builders compare closely with Tenochtitlan's own priest-kings, the Tlatoan, who were likewise self-conscious of time, which they envisioned as the figure of a ferocious sun god. In fact, the chief deity of the Aztecs, the solar Huitzlipochtli, was jointly known as "the Eagle with Arrows of Fire, the Lord of Time."[3]

The people of Aztalan left their ceremonial enclosure, as did the inhabitants of the rest of the walled settlements throughout the Mississippi valley, because their sacred calendar ordered them to do so. Separated by great distances as they were, their alignment posts or sundial pyramids all told their observers the same thing at the same moment: It was time to go. Interestingly, the duration of florescence at Cahokia and the occupation of Aztalan each lasted precisely two centuries. Together, they comprised equal halves of what was defined in the Mesoamerican calendar as the Long Count, a period of four hundred solar years, after which "worlds" (i.e., epochs) came to an end and from which new ones emerged. The sacred calendar strictly regulated the social and even the personal behavior of people in Middle America from known Olmec beginnings (although certainly much earlier, because it appears in their culture already fully developed), in the fourteenth century B.C., through Maya and Toltec times into the Aztec age.

Their lives were absolutely dominated by several intermeshing calendrical cycles, and failure to act in synchronization with their rigidly prescribed dictates could bring ruin to the state or even catastrophe to the whole natural world. The Tonalpohualli was a ritual calendar from which the horoscopes of each person were plotted by astrologers, or Tonalonamatl. The Tonalpouque were yet other priests who determined good and evil days. Merchants, sailors, traders and travelers of all kinds could not begin their journeys until the Tonapouque had determined the proper One Serpent, or Lucky Day. Wars were waged, sacrifices offered, business contracted, marriages made—in truth, social behavior of every kind took place according to the precise instructions of the ritual calendars, as interpreted by ecclesiastic star-gazers.

Operated by every Mesoamerican state, these calendrical systems, for all their astronomical sophistication, were deeply prehistoric, as has been suggested, predating even the oldest recognized Middle American civilizations. As Alfonso Caso writes, "This calendar's development is without doubt very old, and it must have been the creation of a people who attained a high degree of culture prior to that of all the peoples with whose cultures we are now familiar."[4]

At Tikal, in Guatemala, site of one of the very earliest ceremonial cities of the Mayas, colossal pyramids are bunched together, one abutting the next, too many and too close for any conceivable use. They were constructed one after the other, only because the sacred calendar ordered their builders to commence work. And the same calendar was in use in Aztalan.

Dr. James Scherz demonstrated that the Pyramid of the Sun at Aztalan formed a calculated alignment between the top of Pipestone Hill in the west with Christmas Hill in the east to compute sunrise each November 14, which is also the last day or end of the agricultural year in the Maya calendar. November 14 was also the Aztec New Year's Day.

Dr. Scherz was able to show that the North Star figured in prominently among the calculations used by the ancient architects of Aztalan. They needed it to achieve the precision layouts of major earthworks, so it undoubtedly received special recognition in the practice of their sacred geometry. The North Star was similarly honored among the Mayas as Xaman Ek, who was also venerated as the patron of picture writing, perhaps a reference to the written computations that preceded the construction of the earthworks according to his unwavering position in the heavens. Xaman Ek was portrayed in Mayan hieroglyphic script as bearded, always a provocative feature indicative of foreign origins.[5]

The inhabitants of Aztalan and all the other related, although widely separated, fortified towns evacuated in common, because the sacred calendar they universally recognized ordered them to leave at the same time.

"The immediate cause for the abandonment of Spiro," writes Phillips and Brown, "is an historic event that is beyond archaeological reclamation."[6] The same statement may be applied just as appropriately to the dozen or so other ceremonial centers, including Rock Lake-Aztalan, that were vacated around the year 1320.

But if the sacred calendar told the people of Aztalan when to leave, it also told their predecessors when to go to Wisconsin. The Mesoamerican origin of the calendar presumes their Middle American origins as well. So, from the vantage point of millennia, we begin to see the mass migration of whole cultures and populations from south to north and back again as part of the calendrical concept of synchronizing human activity with the movements of the heavens. "As above, so below" is a very old esoteric maxim describing the operation of astrology. In fact, many Plains Indian tribes, such as the Sioux, still regard the South as the beginning and end of all things, where they began and must return.[7]

The absolute origins of the Rock Lake-Aztalan inhabitants are lost in the mythic traditions of Aztlan and with that volcanic island's inescapable resemblance to Plato's Atlantis. But their discernible beginnings start with the Mayas of Yucatan, whose presence at Cahokia and other Mississippian sites cannot be ignored. True, the pyramids throughout Middle America were built of stone, while those in the north are temple-mounds of earth, but stone was not available in sufficiently large quantities and the Mississippians had to work with the materials available to them. Aside from such explicable differences, the Maya impact on North America above the Rio Grande is unmistakable.

Around A.D. 900, the same sacred calendar that had been running the lives of prehistoric Americans for generations ordered them to go north. They resettled in a new city, Cahokia, near the banks of the Mississippi River. Two hundred years later, the solar Long Count reached its midpoint, a highly significant position, in that the time had arrived for them to move north once again and resettle in a new home near Rock Lake's venerated city of the dead. In two more centuries, the Long Count ended and another began, signifying a demand from the sacred calendar to start the grand cycle all over again in its place of origin, in the south.

Judge Hyer was right, back in 1837, when he concluded that the ancient Wisconsinites of Aztalan became the Aztecs. Perhaps he was privy to more information than he divulged, or he may have relied heavily on Native American accounts he was privileged to hear from the Ho Chunk still residing in the Lake Mills area. In any case, the Maya and Cahokian predecessors of the ancient people of Rock Lake-Aztalan are certain.

The removal of the people of Aztalan around A.D. 1320 is a more complex story, but its various elements are no less traceable. They monopolized the mining trade to Middle America, where copper was the basis of the Mesoamerican economy. When local Mexican deposits were discovered, long-distance trade collapsed and Aztalan became commercially superfluous. Coincidental with the end of their status as prosperous miners, the people of Aztalan were internally torn by a religious controversy and externally beset by a prolonged drought. They probably did not need to be told by their astronomer-priests reading from the sacred calendar that the moment had come for them to depart. They may have interpreted that providential calendrical demand in the light of their concomitant misfortunes, as the will of heaven, and willingly deserted Aztalan to seek their destiny in the southland of their ancestors. And so the mass abandonment took place according to the cycles of time they had recognized and lived by for unguessed generations.

•Summary•

Five Thousand Years
in One Thousand Words

A t a time when Egypt's first pharaoh sat on the falcon-throne—when
the Near East represented the only known civilized territories on
earth—fleets of European seafarers from islands in the Atlantic
braved the ocean toward North America. They sailed through what is now
the St. Lawrence Seaway, more accessible five thousand years ago than it is
today. Cruising further westward into the Great Lakes, they made for the
Upper Peninsula, the world's greatest source of high-grade copper and the
object of their long voyage. How they knew it abounded there is a question
lost to prehistory.

The visitors disembarked at Isle Royale and along the Keweenau Peninsula, setting up fair-weather mining camps and sinking pit mines into the
hard, rocky ground. They excavated tons of the mineral, loading the holds
of their ships with raw copper, then traveled the inland waterways south to
a clearing-house just below the hard snow line, in southern Wisconsin, at
a small lake named after one of their leading families, Tirajana. Here the

stored copper was processed into ingots, while the miners waited out the winter until late spring or early summer when the mines were reopened. Imposing structures—stone sundials, oriented mounds, alignment posts, etc.—were built to provide them with accurate calendrical information for the planting and harvesting of crops, sailing schedules, mining timetables and more. Science combined with religion as the most honored dead were entombed beneath the astronomical monuments, which also served as shrines for a mystery cult. The lake shore became a sprawling cemetery, a necropolis, or City of the Dead, with settlements throughout the immediate vicinity.

The copper ingots were loaded aboard ships that navigated the Rock River to the Mississippi, into the Gulf of Mexico and back across the sea to the Atlantic homeland. Its oceanic capital achieved tremendous prosperity as the major supplier of copper to Bronze Age societies throughout Europe and the Near East for 1,800 years. Meanwhile, Wisconsin's Tirajana continued to function as a strategically located mining town, and its fame spread for the important ceremonial center it had become.

But in the twelfth century B.C., the Michigan mines were shut down and Tirajana's residents prepared to leave. Relations with the native Paleo-Indian population had not been consistently amicable, so, to protect the necropolis from desecration, a canal was opened from the river running due north of Tirajana, inundating most of the sacred precinct under sixty feet of water. As the disenfranchised miners fled southward, some were massacred by ancestors of the Attiwandeton and Chippewas. At least a few attempted a transatlantic voyage to Europe. Others went further south, sparking or at least impacting Mesoamerican civilizations, establishing their all-pervasive religion based on the cycles of time and eventually intermarrying with the natives.

Around A.D. 900, their descendants, the Ecuadoran Canari, introduced hard currency in the form of copper "axe-monies" to Middle and South American societies and reopened the mines of their forefathers in Michigan's Upper Peninsula. A new mining center was established in southwest Illinois, known today as Cahokia. It flourished near the Mississippi River as a great commercial enterprise, dispatching its miners north in summer and shipping tons of precious copper south to fuel the economies of Mesoamerica and the Andes. Two hundred years later, Cahokia's astronomer-priests, interpreting the sacred calender, ordered the city abandoned. Its residents scattered by tribes throughout the Mississippi valley and the South, raising similar, Cahokia-like settlements. One of the larger contingents migrated north to the sacred lake remembered as Tyranena and built an observatory town three miles to the east, Aztalan. Tyranena's shores were again used for burials, while the few, ruinous stone structures still standing above the surface of the water on little islands were once more venerated as shrines and holy places. Mining operations in Michigan were perpetuated, while the people of Aztalan oversaw the storage and processing of the copper into ox hide ingots before their shipment down the Rock and Mississippi Rivers to Middle and South America.

But in the first quarter of the fourteenth century, native Mexican copper deposits were discovered. The Great Lakes' sources were no longer needed, its mines were once more shut down and Aztalan lost its economic reason for being. Coincidental with the copper crisis, sustained drought afflicted southern Wisconsin, while a religious schism generated social chaos within the ceremonial center. Moreover, the sacred calendar informed its residents that they had completed a four-hundred-year cycle known as the Long Count and that the moment had come for them to leave. Convinced that their misfortunes were the results of a cannibalistic death-cult they allowed to flourish behind its high walls, the inhabitants incinerated Aztalan in a ritualized conflagration to purge the desecrated sacred center. They migrated south into the Valley of Mexico, where, in A.D. 1325, they built the city of Tenochtitlan, from which they developed and ruled the Aztec Empire until the Spanish Conquest two hundred years later.

In the 1830s, the first modern European settlers in southern Wisconsin erected mills and dams that raised Tyranena's water levels between seven and twenty feet, submerging whatever ancient monuments may still have stood above the surface. Henceforward known as Rock Lake, the structures survived only in legend until 1900, when they were seen during another drought. In 1937, Max Nohl, inventor of the scuba, found a cone-shaped structure in the south end of the lake. Thirty years later, a diving instructor, John Kennedy, discovered a large, tent-shaped pyramid toward the center. During the 1980s, Dr. James Scherz calculated the astronomical significance of Aztalan, and, in the last years of the decade, the first side-scan sonar search of Rock Lake revealed effigy mounds and several other man-made features on the bottom. In 1991, the first distinguishable photographs of an underwater monument were made, prompting action to have Rock Lake declared a historical site by the State of Wisconsin. More than ten years later, that official protection of the lake and its sunken city of the dead is still withheld.

Art by Kenneth Caroli

Notes

Chapter 1: The Search Begins

1. Mary M. Wilson, *A History of Lake Mills* (Madison, WI: Omnipress, 1983), 543.

2. Margaret Krueger, "Legend of Pyramids in Lake Gaining Credibility," *Watertown Daily Times*, Aug. 29, 1991.

3. Wilson, *History of Lake Mills*, 541.

4. *The Milwaukee Herald,* 20 Aug. 1900.

5. Helen Mansfield, "Everyone Knows How to Find Bartels," *Janesville Gazette*, June 2, 1960.

6. Paul Gericke, *History of Lake Mills* (Lake Mills, WI: Feb. 13, 1936), 66

7. Ibid.

8. Wilson, *History of Lake Mills*, 545.

9. *The Lake Mills Leader,* Aug. 7, 1952.

10. Max Gene Nohl, personal letter to Victor Taylor, Oct. 12, 1937, Historical Archives File Folder, L. D. Fargo Library, Lake Mills, WI.

11. Ibid.

12. Ibid.

13. Wilson, *History of Lake Mills*, 544.

14. *The Lake Mills Leader,* Aug. 7, 1952.

15. *The Lake Mills Leader,* June 2, 1960.

16. *The Wisconsin Archaeologist,* Fall 1962, 7.

17. Ben Whitcomb, "The Lost Pyramids of Rock Lake," *Skin Diver* (January 1970): 24, 25, 84.

18. T. M. Spencer, "Lake Mills' Controversy: Pyramids or Pyramidal?" *Underwater U.S.A.* (February 1966).

19. Dr. James P. Scherz, Rock Lake Underwater Survey, Annex A, "Search of Historical Data," June 10, 1989, Madison, WI.

Chapter 2: Exploration and Discovery

1. Ben Whitcomb, "The Lost Pyramids of Rock Lake," *Skin Diver* (January 1970): 24, 25, 84.

2. Frank Joseph, "Wisconsin's Frightening Sacred Center," *Fate* (October 1991).

3. "Pyramids Sighted," *Daily Jefferson County Union,* Apr. 1, 1988.

4. Klein Associates, Inc., Undersea Search and Survey, Klein Drive, Salem, NH 03079.

5. Craig Scott, President, Sea Search, Inc., 2445 East Hile Road, Muskegon, MI 49444

6. Frank Joseph, "Found: The Lost Pyramids of Rock Lake," *Fate* (September 1989).

7. P. F. Strauss, *Society in Ancient Greece and Asia Minor* (Boston, MA: Richardson Publishers, 1900), 121

8. Betty Sodders, *Michigan Prehistory Mysteries, Volume II* (AuTrain, MI: Avery Color Studios, 1991), 102.

Chapter 3: The Veil Parts

1. Eagle, P.O. Box 669, Catoosa, OK 74015-0669

Chapter 5: Ancient Pyramid or Glacial Debris?

1. T. M. Spencer, "Lake Mills' Controversy: Pyramids or Pyramidal?" *Underwater USA,* Feb. 1966.

2. Ibid.

3. Dr. James P. Scherz, *Rock Lake Underwater Survey,* Madison, WI: June 1989.

Chapter 6: The Evidence Speaks for Itself

1. Bence-Albee Analysis, "Deposit on Rock,"(Chicago: Geological Sciences, University of Illinois, VHS Log 1-10.240, 09:28, Aug. 24, 1989).

2. S. A. Barrett, *Ancient Aztalan,* vol. XIII of *Bulletin of the Public Museum of the City of Milwaukee* (Milwaukee, WI: 1933).

Chapter 8: How Did the Pyramids Sink?

1. Robert Laskey, "Rock Lake's Pyramid," *Wisconsin Gazette,* 1940.

2. Dr. Franz Kirschner, "Tree Ring Dating of the Middle Mississippian Epoch," *American Archaeology Today* (Fall 1959).

3. H.R. Hannover, *Native Legends of the Great Lakes* (New York: Wireton Press, 1889).

Chapter 10: Native Americans Remember the Pyramid Drama

1. Robert Vollbrech, *Indian Histories* (New York: MacMillan Company, 1960).

Chapter 11: The Monster of Rock Lake

1. Mary M. Wilson, *A History of Lake Mills* (Madison, WI: Omnipress, 1983), 522.

2. Ibid., 521.

3. James Brandon, *Weird America* (New York: E.P. Dutton, 1978), 242-246.

4. Dr. Donald Roberts, *Secret of the Stone* (London: Faber & Faber, 1990).

5. Paul Deveraux, *The Dragon Project* (London: Heresfield, Ltd., 1989).

6. Betty Sodders, *Michigan Prehistory Mysteries, Vol. II* (AuTrain, MI: Avery Color Studios, 1991).

7. Charles E. Brown, in *The Wisconsin Archaeologist*, V:4 (Sept. 1926).

Chapter 12: The Great Copper Mystery

1. Octave DuTemple, ed., articles (Calumet, MI, 1961).

2. William P.F. Ferguson, "Michigan's Most Ancient Industry: The Prehistoric Mines and Miners of Isle Royale," in articles, Octave du Temple, ed., 1961.

3. Roy W. Drier, "Prehistoric Mining in the Copper Country," in articles, Octave du Temple, ed., 1961.

4. Ibid.

5. Angus Murdoch, *Boom Copper* (New York: The MacMillan Company, 1943), 127.

6. Ibid., 202.

7. W. H. Holmes, "Aboriginal Copper Mines of Isle Royale, Lake Superior," *American Anthropologist*, III (1901): 684.

8. Roy W. Drier, "Prehistoric Mining in the Copper Country," in articles, Octave du Temple, ed., 1961.

9. S. A. Barrett, "Ancient Aztalan," *Bulletin of the Public Museum of the City of Milwaukee*, XIII (1933): 173.

10. Charles E. Brown, "Rock Lake," *The Wisconsin Archaeologist*, V:4 (Sept. 1926).

Chapter 13: Revelation in the Canary Islands

1. John Harms, *Romance and Truth in the Canary Islands* (Phoenix, AZ: Acorn Press, 1965), 127, 128.

2. Ibid., 105.

3. Professor Lopez Herrera, *The Canary Islands*, trans. Michael Kelly (Madrid: Municipal Publishers, 1989), 76.

4. Ibid., 84.

5. Ibid., 89.

6. Ibid., 101.

7. James Breasted, *Ancient Records of Egypt* (Chicago, IL: University of Chicago Press, 1905), 183.

8. Lynne Goldstein (University of Wisconsin [Madison]) and Joan E. Freeman (State Historical Society of Wisconsin), *A Walking Tour of Aztalan* (Aztalan Park Fund, c/o Gordon Roglitz, Route 2, Jefferson, WI 53549), 1990.

9. Glen Black, *Angel Site, Vol. II* (Indianapolis: University of Indiana Press, 1965), 142.

10. Betty Sodders, *Michigan Prehistory Mysteries, Vol. II* (AuTrain, MI: Avery Color Studios, 1991), 137.

11. James Robert Enterline, *Viking America* (New York: Doubleday and Company, 1972), 111.

12. Ibid., 110, 111.

13. Bartoleme de la Casas, *Journal of the First Voyage of Columbus*, Collection of John Cabot, ed. Edward Gaylord Bourne, Yale (New York: Barnes and Noble, 1976. Reprint of Charles Scribners and Sons 1906 edition), 93.

14. Ibid., page 100.

15. Ibid., page 97.

16. Ignatius Donnelly, *Atlantis, the Antediluvian World* (New York: Harper and Brothers, 1882), 178.

17. Dorothy Hosler, Heather Lechtman and Olaf Holm, *Axe-Monies and Their Relatives*, no. 30 of *Studies in Prehistoric Art and Archaeology* (Washington, D. C.: Dumbarton Oaks Research Library and Collection, 1990).

18. Dr. R.W. Pruett, *Gods and Demons of South American Mythology* (New York: Richter Publishing Company, 1948), 39.

19. Enterline, *Viking America,* 107.

20. Albert B. Donworth, *Why Columbus Sailed* (New York: Exposition Press, 1953), 98.

21. Vilhjalmur Stefansson, *The Friendly Arctic* (New York: Macmillan Company, 1921), 142.

22. Enterline, *Viking America,* 102.

23. Ibid.

24. Dr. James P. Scherz, *Rock Lake Underwater Survey* (Madison, WI: June 1989).

Chapter 14: The Serpent People

1. John Pinsent, *Greek Mythology* (London: Hamlyn, 1969).

2. Ibid.

3. Genesis IV:8.

4. Peter Vollmer, *Anatolian Archaeology* (New York: E.P. Dutton, 1960), 158.

5. Maitland A. Edey, *The Sea Traders* (New York: Time-Life Books, 1974).

Chapter 15: Aztalan, the Profaned Sacred Center

1. Lester Crown, *Fantastic Animals* (New York: Doubleday and Company, 1971), 55.

2. Increase Lapham, *The Antiquities of Wisconsin,* vol. IV of *Antiquities of the New World: Early Explorations in Archaeology* (Cambridge, MA: A.M.S. Press, for the Peabody Museum of Archaeology and Ethnology, Harvard University, 1973 reprint of 1853 original), 46.

3. S. A. Barrett, "Ancient Aztalan," *Bulletin of the Public Museum of the City of Milwaukee, Wisconsin,* XIII (1933), 151.

4. Ibid., 53.

5. Ibid., 77.

6. Reuben G. Thwaites,vol. V of *The Jesuit Relations and Allied Document,* (Cleveland, OH: 1901).

7. Barrett, *Ancient Aztalan,* 48.

Chapter 16: Tyranena, Sunken City of the Dead

1. Letter to Victor Taylor, Oct. 12, 1937, at the L. D. Fargo Public Library, Lake Mills, WI.

2. Charles E. Brown, "Rock Lake," *The Wisconsin Archaeologist,* V:4 (Sept.1926).

3. Ibid.

4. George Bauer, *Myths of the Great Lakes Indians* (Chicago: Frontier Publications, 1940), 103.

Chapter 18: The Aztec Connection

1. Robert Silverberg, *The Mound Builders* (New York: MacMillan, 1975).

2.Glen Black, *Angel Site,* vol.II (Indianapolis: University of Indiana Press, 1965), 53.

3. S. A. Barrett, "Ancient Aztalan," *Bulletin of the Public Museum of the City of Milwaukee, Wisconsin,* XIII (1933), 153.

4. Ibid., 184.

5. Lynne Goldstein (University of Wisconsin [Madison]) and Joan E. Freeman (State Historical Society of Wisconsin), *A Walking Tour of Aztalan* (Aztalan Park Fund, c/o Gordon Roglitz, Route 2, Jefferson, WI 53549), 1990.

6. Moundsville Museum of Archaeology, Moundsville, Ohio.

7. Old Stone Fort Museum of Archaeology, Old Stone Fort Archaeological Area, Bedford County, Tennessee.

8. Barrett, "Ancient Aztalan," 122.

9. C. A. Burland, *Myths of the Aztecs* (Boston: Faber and Faber, 1977), 33.

10. S. A. Barrett, "Ancient Aztalan," *Bulletin of the Public Museum of the City of Milwaukee, Wisconsin,* XIII (1933), 92.

11. *Aztalan, the Site at Merrom,* Sullivan County Archives, 1940, Public Museum of Indianapolis, Indiana.

12. Burland, *Myths of the Aztecs,* 73.

13. Lewis H. Morgan, *Ancient Society* (Chicago: Charles H. Kerr and Company, 1877), 194.

14. Alfonso Caso, *The Aztecs: People of the Sun* (Norman, OK: University of Oklahoma Press, 1958), 127.

15. Ibid., 58.

16. Black, *Angel Site,* 42.

17. Morgan, *Ancient Society,* 195.

18. Ibid., 196.

19. Ake Hultkranz, *The Religion of the American Indians* (Berkeley, C A: University of California Press, 1979), 276, 277.

20. Leslie and Peter T. Furst, *Pre-Columbian Art of Mexico* (New York: Abbeville Press, 1980), 87.

21. Sylvanus Griswold Moreley, *An Introduction to the Study of the Maya Hieroglyphs* (New York: Dover Publications, Inc., 1976), 12.

22. Hultkranz, *Religion of the American Indians,* 176.

Chapter 19: Axe-Money

1. Dorothy Hosler, Heather Lechtman and Olaf Holm, *Axe-Monies and their Relatives,* no. 30 of *Studies in Prehistoric Art and Archaeology* (Washington, D.C.: Dumbarton Oaks Research Library and Collection, 1990).

2. Ibid.

3. Victor von Hagen, *The Aztec Man and Tribe* (New York: The New American Library, 1961).

4. Betty Sodders, *Michigan Prehistory Mysteries, Vol. II* (AuTrain, MI: Avery Color Studios, 1991), 147.

5. Hosler et al., *Axe-Monies and their Relatives.*

6. Ibid.

7. F. W. Kraus, *The Sun and the Serpent* (New York: Lippincott Publishers, 1970), 44.

8. Dr. William Prang, *Meteorological History* (Boston: Horizon Publishers, 1969) 206.

Chapter 20: The Lord of Time

1. Alfonso Ortiz, "Through Tewa Eyes," *National Geographic,* 180:4 (Oct. 1991), 7.

2. Ibid.

3. Alfonso Caso, *The Aztecs: People of the Sun,* (Norman, OK: University of Oklahoma Press, 1958), 67.

4. Ibid., 69.

5. Sylvanus Griswold Moreley, *An Introduction to the Study of the Maya Hieroglyphs* (New York: Dover Publications, 1975), 18.

6. Phillip Phillips and James A. Brown, *Pre-Columbian Shell Engravings from the Craig Mound at Spiro, Oklahoma,* vol. I (Cambridge, MA: Peabody Museum Press, Peabody Museum of Archaeology and Ethnology, Harvard University, 1984), 21.

7. Joe Epps Brown, *The Sacred Pipe* (Norman, OK: University of Oklahoma Press, 1989), 20.

To order additional copies of this book,
please send full amount plus $4.00 for
postage and handling for the first book and
50¢ for each additional book.

Send orders to:

Galde Press, Inc.
PO Box 460
Lakeville, Minnesota 55044-0460

Credit card orders call 1–800–777–3454
Phone (952) 891–5991 • Fax (952) 891–6091
Visit our website at www.galdepress.com

Write for our free catalog.